The *Khat* Conundrum in Ethiopia:

Socioeconomic Impacts and Policy Directions

Yeraswork Admassie

Forum for Social Studies (FSS)

Addis Ababa

FSS Monograph No. 12

ISBN: 978-99944-50-63-3

Forum for Social Studies (FSS)
P.O. Box 25864 code 1000
Addis Ababa, Ethiopia
Email: fss@ethionet.et
Web: www.fssethiopia.org.et

This Monograph has been published with the financial support of the Civil Societies Support Program (CSSP). The contents of the Monograph are the sole responsibilities of the author and can under no circumstances be regarded as reflecting the position of the CSSP or the FSS.

Contents

Acknowledgements

The preparation of the report would not have been possible without the valuable contributions and support of many individuals and organizations.

In particular, I wish to express my deep gratitude to Ato Ezana Amdework, Department of Sociology, AAU, for his diligent assistance in organizing and conducting the collection of data throughout the fieldwork in both Assosa and Harar, Dr Asnake Kefale, Adjunct Researcher at FSS, for his thorough review of the draft monograph leading to a good number of basic improvements.

I also wish to thank the following organizations, their managements and personnel from Assosa profound appreciation for facilitating the fieldworks on three occasions and for providing valuable information on their work:

Civil Society Support Program (CSSP) Western (Ethiopia) Regional Business Unit: Ato Jebessa Senbeta, Manager, Ato Abdi Begna, Officer;

- Benishangul-Gumuz Development Association Network (BGDAN): Ato Fantahun Meless, Executive Director, Ato Belay Zeleke, Program Coordinator, Ato Ashenafi Berhanu, M&E Officer;
- Assosa Environmental Protection Association (AEPA):Ato Mengistu Bayssa, Manager, Ato Mola Berhe, Field Officer;
- Tesfa Belechta Association (TBA): Ato Habtamu Tamiru, Manager, Ato Hassan Ali, Program Officer;
- Mao-Komo Development Association: Ato Sultan Hailu, Executive Director; Education for Development Association: Ato Chimdessa Negero, Program Coordinator;
- Mujuju Waloca (Women Development) Association; and
- Mental Health Department of Assosa General Hospital: Ato Derbachew Melkamu, Chief Psychiatrist.

Likewise, I am thankful to the following organizations, their managements and personnel from Harar, for facilitating the fieldworks on two occasions and for providing valuable information on their activities:

- CSSP Eastern (Ethiopia) Regional Business Unit: Ato Tadesse Negash, Manager, and Wz. Beza Sileshi, Program Coordinator;
- Ethiopian Youth Network – Harari Branch (EYNHB): Ato Muktar Ali, General Manager and Wz. Sara Mohammad, Cashier;
- Harari *Iddïr* and Afosha Coalition (HIAC): Ato Hailu Bekele, Chairperson, and Ato Wuhib Mohammad;
- Stand for Integrated Development - Ethiopia (SID-E): Ato Selamyihun Aklilu, Executive Director;
- The Steering Committee on *Khat* Addiction and Prevention: Ato Abduwassi, Vice-chairperson; and
- Hiwot Fana Specialized University Hospital: Ato Habtamu Tadesse, Psychiatrist, and Wz. Aster Mulugeta, Psychiatric Nurse.

Similarly, I am indebted to the four-and-half dozen informants in Assosa and Harar who willingly and openly shared some general and other personal information through key-informant interviews and focus-group discussions/interviews. The names of these informants are not listed here in order to avoid unnecessary repetition, since they appear either in full or in initials -- the latter, in order to protect their privacy in cases where the information is too personal -- in the monograph, which in no way lessens the acknowledgement due to them.

Last, but not least, my special thanks go to the study's national-level informants. In particular, I am grateful to Dr Mesfin Araya, Dr Solomon Tefera and Dr Yonas Baheretibeb, Associate Professors of Psychiatry, College of Health Sciences, AAU; as well as Commander Tsegaye Woldemehret, Head of the Dangerous Drugs Circulation Control Division of the Federal Police; Ato Dawit Dikasso Advisor to the Director General, FMHACA; and Ato Damtew Alemu, Team Leader, MoLSA; for their valuable inputs made through interviews and/or during the National Conference held on 1-2 April 2016.

Obviously, in spite of their generous contributions, none of the above mentioned organizations and individuals share the burden of responsibility for any possible errors and omissions in the work. These lie exclusively with the author.

Preface

This work is a product of long duration. A study on *Khat* was generally envisage some two decades ago together with the establishment of the Forum for Social Studies, as part of a larger research program on substance abuse that included a second one on *Araké*. The latter study was undertaken in 2009-10 and its findings published as *the Araké Dilemma: The Socioeconomics of Traditional Distilled Alcohol Production, Marketing, and Consumption in Ethiopia*. In the introduction to that work, we had already written as follows:

> ... A few negative social phenomena of relatively recent origin have begun eroding [the country's] human resource base and overstretching its limited social services. Such is the case with the galloping addiction to, and abuse of, substances, of which the most prominent are *c'at* and home-distilled alcohol, the spread of pornographic dens and gambling hangouts.

> Yet, Ethiopian society, like many others in the developing world, has ignored the issue of substance abuse. Instead of addressing the issue, the Government, for instance, has passively encouraged the cultivation, marketing and consumption of *c'at*, because of its importance as a source of cash income to many farmers and its significance as a major foreign currency earner to the nation (Yeraswork Admassie and Ezana Amdework, 2010: 1).

Yet, in spite of the urgency for research on *Khat* that was expressed seven years ago, the present study had to wait until 2015 for an opportune moment that made conditions for data collection ripe. Now that it is completed, I can confidently say that the dream of investigating the two socioeconomic hazards of Ethiopian society, namely, *Araké* that is by and large spreading from its centers in the North and the central parts of the country to the southern and south-eastern regions as it also moves from rural to urban areas, and *Khat*, which is engulfing the central, western, and northern part of the country leapfrogging from the East as it also moves from urban to rural.

The study focused on the socioeconomic impacts of *Khat* consumption and addiction, as well as efforts that are underway to curb the spread of *Khat* consumption and addiction in Harar and Assosa, with the ultimate aim of contributing toward the formulation of appropriate policy and the preparation of feasible strategies to prevent the spread of addiction as well as to redress the damage already done. In recent years, there has been a rapid expansion of *Khat* production, marketing and consumption, and together with these, an escalation of problems associated with addiction to the substance. *Khat* addiction has led to multifaceted socio-economic problems. It has created stress in household income and income distribution; destructs children and youth from education; and created numerous health problems. *Khat* addiction among the youth and children would have wider implication not only for the individuals and their families, but also for the country as a whole.

This qualitative study aimed at learning about the socioeconomic impacts of *Khat* through the perceptions of various categories of the residents of Harar and Assosa Cities and Federal-level authorities and institutions as well as through the field observation of the researcher. By generating primary data, it has identified trends of *Khat* consumption and addiction at different levels – household (family), community and countrywide. It has also assessed interventions that are underway by government and non-governmental actors in order to reverse the current trend. The study attempts to provide insights that would help to develop effective pathways for intervention by governmental agencies and non-governmental actors including civil society organizations (CSOs), community based organizations, businesses and others.

The main study strategy and the reporting style that are followed were guided by the belief that much can be learned about *Khat* through the voices of the people who are directly and indirectly affected, those who are trying to do something about it, as well as experts and officials who are active or passive witness of whatever is going on. To that effect, individual cases and stories that are capable of providing insight into the problem and its solution better than any second hand reporting are presented in a number of individuals' case stories in separate entries or boxes. The author hopes that this approach will provide the reader with insightful and genuine narrative.

The draft report of this study, together with several other papers, was presented and discussed at a two-day National Conference held on 12 & 13 April 2016 and attended by stakeholders and experts. Since, important players from the

Cities of Assosa and Harar were in attendance, the Conference also acted as a validation workshop for the study contributing toward its improvement and finalization. Moreover, deliberations at the National Conference provided inputs that greatly contributed towards the preparation of the closing chapter of this volume that deals with proposed national-level policy intervention to tackle the *Khat* conundrum.

The First Chapter of this volume presents the background, objectives, and methods, sources of informants, rationale and scope of the study. The Second chapter is dedicated to the presentation of the findings of the study concerning (a) socioeconomic impacts of *Khat* (b) attempts that are underway to reverse the escalating spread of *Khat* consumption and addiction, and (3) the experiences of, and journeys traversed by those who were *Khat* addicts as they got into and then escaped from the clutches dependence and addiction, or as they struggle to do so in Assosa. The Third Chapter does the same for Harar. The Fourth Chapter offers an examination of the contextual factors that need to be taken into consideration in the search for a viable national response to the *Khat* crisis and proceeds to propose and sketch a viable alternative pathway for the formulation of policy and intervention strategy in order to hinder the spread of *Khat* consumption and addiction at the national level. The Fifth Chapter ends the work with certain concluding remarks.

The field research of the study, the finding of which is reported in this volume, was conducted with the facilitation of CSSP and its grantee CSOs both in Assosa and Harar. The study was carried out under the auspices of the Forum for Social Studies, which is an independent think-tank of long standing, and hence it represents an impartial and balanced investigation that was only guided by the principle of seeking truth from facts.

Finally, an explanatory note on a single nomenclature is due. In this work both Harar and Assosa are referred to as 'city' and not 'town', notwithstanding their small population size which is even truer in the case of the latter. The decision to opt for the term 'city' in both cases was based on two considerations. The first concerns the fact that both are equally the capitals of their respective National Regional States, and therefore to label them differently on the basis of size alone would ignore the other criterion for differentiating between settlements, which is administrative function. The second reason for opting to refer to them as 'city' was to pay heed to the trend which is likely to make them develop into veritable cities in the foreseeable future anyways. One can also add, with guarded sarcasm, that if Sir Richard Burton could call the Harar of the 1850s a metropolis, wouldn't it be safe to grant it the rank of a city now at the beginning of the 21st Century?

Acronyms

AAU	Addis Ababa University
AEPA	Assosa Environmental Protection Association
BGDAN	Benishangul-Gumuz Development Association Network
BoE	Bureau of Education
BoH	Bureau of Health
BoLSA	Bureau of Labor and Social Affairs
BoWCYA	Bureau of Women, Children and Youth Affairs
CBO	Community Based Organization
CCC	Community Care Coalition
CSA	Central Statistics Agency (of Ethiopia)
CS-FGD	Civil Society - Focus Group Discussion
CSO	Civil Society Organization
CSSP	Civil Society Support Program (of DFID)
DDT	Dichlorodiphenyltrichloroethane
DFID	Department For International Development (United Kingdom)
EDA	Education for Development Association
EDHS	Ethiopian Demographic and Health Survey
ERHS	Ethiopia Rural Household Survey
ETOC	Ethiopian Tewahedo Orthodox Church
EYNHB	Ethiopian Youth Network – Harari Branch
FDG	Focus Group Discussion
FDG/I	Focus Group Discussion/Interview
FMHACA	Food, Medicine and Health Care Administration and Control Authority
FSS	Forum for Social Studies
GTP-II	Growth and Transformation Plan II

HIAC	Harari Ïddïr and Afosha Coalition
IGA	Income Generating Activity
KII	Key Informant Interview
M&E	Monitoring and Evaluation
MoE	Ministry of Education
MoFEC	Ministry of Finance and Economic Cooperation
MoH	Ministry of Health
MoLSA	Ministry of Labor and Social Affairs
MSE	Micro and Small Enterprise
NGO	Non Governmental Organization
NRS	National Regional State
OoCWYA	Office of Women, Children and Youth Affairs (*Wäräda*)
SID-E	Stand for Integrated Development - Ethiopia
SPG	Strategic Partnership Grant (of CSSP/DFID)
TB	Tuberculosis
TBA	Tesfa Belechta Association
TVET	Technical and Vocational Education and Training
VAT	Value added Tax
UNODC	United Nations Office on Drug and Crime

List of Plates

List of Tables

List of Boxes

1   Introduction

1.1   Background

Available factual data and the public's perception are in agreement on one important issue. In these, opening decades of the 21st Century, Ethiopia is experiencing a veritable deluge —that of a small shrub plant that is exponentially invading its agricultural lands and the minds of its people and goes by the names of *Khat, Č'at, Chat, Qat, Gaad, Miraa, etc*. There is no denying that *Khat* plant has been famously in use for centuries in some parts of Ethiopia, particularly Harar and its surroundings, to the extent that the area is considered to be its birthplace by many early writers including the famous traveler, Sir Richard Burton (1856, Vol. I, Preface to the 1856 edition: xxvi). But, in recent years its production has boomed and its consumption escalated to pandemic levels. So also, it has made headway from its traditional homelands into areas where it was once unknown and its use was a virtual taboo.

Before the 1950s, the production of *Khat* was a relatively small-scale activity, limited to certain parts of the country. Recently, and particularly during the last one-and-half decade, however, its production has experienced a surge that raised its cultivation area by 160% and its annual production by 243%. *Khat* is now grown on one quarter million hectares of land, which is 44% of the land under coffee (CSA, 2015). The increasing importance of *Khat* as a form of asset dear to farmers is indicated by the fact that almost a fifth of the country's rural households were found to grow the plant in 2011 (CSA. 2012b: Table 9.1, b).

Table 1 below makes very clear the levels and alarming trends of *Khat* production in the seven Regional States of the country excluding Tigray and Afar for which data were unavailable:

The market for *Khat* has also shown astronomic growth being driven by a large consumer base and surging disposable income. *Khat* has thus become prominent in both the country's domestic and foreign trade, coming second only to coffee as the country's most important foreign currency earner by bringing in nearly 300 million USD (Cochrane, L., and D. O'Regan, 2016). The Growth and Transformation Plan-II that is currently in its second year of implementation, foresees the value of the annual export of *Khat* to grow from 272.4 million USD in the base year of 2014/15 to 650.8

million USD in 2019/20, which represents an increase of 58.1% over the five years duration of the plan (GTP-II, Table 2.5: 104).

Table 1: Regions of Rapid *Khat* Production, in Hectares (2003/04–2014/15)

Region	2003/04	2014/15	Percentage Increase
Amhara	2,718	9,563	252%
Benishangul-Gumuz	46	1,183	2,471%
Dire Dawa	713	1,325	86%
Gambella	39	393	908%
Harari	2,038	4,844	138%
Oromia	75,196	156,522	108%
SNNP	22,570	69,505	208%

Source: Reproduced from Cochrane and O'Regan (2016: 2) that is based on CSA (2004–2015) data.[1]

Its domestic consumption, too, has skyrocketed during the same period. Next to coffee, *Khat* is now the most frequently used stimulant in the country. The 2011 Ethiopian Demographic & Health Survey (EDHS) throws light on the prevalence of *Khat* consumption in the country. Unfortunately, neither the 2000 nor the 2005 EDHS make a similar query on *Khat* consumption, denying us the advantage of comparison to gauge the direction and the rate at which change has been taking place. Nonetheless, 2011 EDHS found that in the country as a whole 27.6% of all men and 11.0% of all women who are 15-49 years old have ever chewed *Khat*. It also revealed that 50.0% of the men and 43.1% of the women that have ever chewed *Khat*, have done so for more than 6 times within the 30 days' duration preceding the survey.

The commercial supply of *Khat* in large urban centers has also undergone a process of "modernization" and "adornment". In Addis Ababa, it is served in high-class chewing cum entertainment parlors; and motorbike bound *Khat* delivery services are becoming commonplace. Decorative billboards advertising choice-*Khat* of specific localities and shops line some of the streets of city, even being used as covers of the protective

---

[1] The authors have attached the following explanatory note that may be useful in appreciating the table: "Note that this earliest regional data we were able to access started at this point. However, national data from 2001/02 was available, thus national figures listed in the paper refer to 2001/02 while this regional data refers to 2003/04. Data for Harari region is from 2013/14, as the 2014/15 data was unavailable".

fencings of streetside trees planted by the City Government —apparently, with the latter's blessings. *Khat* is placed on a pedestal of legitimate business and celebrated as the "in thing".

Furthermore, *Khat* consumption is omnipresent across Ethiopia's regional states, albeit in varying degrees. The same 2011 EDHS has shown the wide regional differences that exist concerning *Khat* consumption, varying from 81.9% and 39.2% for the men and women in Harari to 3.7% and 0.9 % for those in Tigray. Latecomer regions such as Benishangul-Gumuz fall in between the two extremes, with 18.7% of the men and 3.3% of the women having ever chewed *Khat* and 18.0% and 7.9% of these, respectively, reporting to have chewed it for more than six times in the course of the 30 days preceding the survey (CSA, 2012a, Tables 3.10.1&2: 54-55).

The consumption of *Khat* in contemporary Ethiopia knows no social boundary. Males and females, as well as persons of all geographical areas, age groups, religious denomination, income and educational status, in short, members of all social groups feature among *Khat* chewers in varying numbers. Yet, of all the social groups affected by *Khat* consumption (addiction), the increase in *Khat* consumption and addiction among the youth and children is exceptional. *Khat* habituation and addiction are rolling like a juggernaut through the ranks of the Ethiopian youth. For instance, according to one study, the prevalence of *Khat* consumption and addiction among high school students is 15% in Shashemene and Hawassa City (Gete Tesgaye, 2007 EC) and 18% in Dire Dawa (Binyam Negussie *et al,* 2014). The phenomenon has thus become so worrying that it was made the specific subject of a recently published popular Amharic book appropriately titled 'the Youth and *Khat*' (ወልደአማኑኤል ጉዳሶ፤ ጥር 2007 እ.ኢ.አ. (2015).

In spite of the fact that several millions of its citizens are preoccupied with *Khat* in the capacities of growers, traders, and chewers, the country has no clear policy to guide its production, distribution or use. To date, neither of them is legally sanctioned, regulated or forbidden. The rule of the game appears to be one of benign neglect. As long as it continues to serve the country by bringing in hundreds of millions of USD, supporting the livelihood of millions of farming households, and keeping its local consumers happy and satisfied, the show is likely to be allowed to go on without any meaningful intervention.

Thus, Ethiopian society in general, and the government of the day in particular, find themselves in a double bind concerning *Khat*. They are under the iron grip of *Khat* in the same way as millions of the addicts who languish under its the spell, since its export generates valuable hard currency to the country's economy and millions of farmers depend on it for their livelihood.

Thus, in spite of its widespread production and consumption and the resultant socioeconomic problems that addicts and their families face, there is a dearth of up-to-date research on the perception and awareness of the socioeconomic impacts of *Khat*, and what could be done to reverse the escalating *Khat* consumption/addiction as well as to rehabilitate those who are already addicted to it. Hence, it is imperative that policy-oriented research on *Khat* be undertaken with the specific purpose of contributing towards addressing these lacunae.

i.   Helping in identifying pathways for constructive intervention by governmental agencies, civil society organizations (CSOs), and other relevant actors to prevent and limit youth addiction and thereby contribute towards the institutionalization of appropriate regulatory framework that would promote the prevention of addiction by regional and federal government authorities; and

ii.   Ameliorating the situation of those negatively affected by *Khat* addiction and to help them to become free from the addiction.

1.2   Conceptualization of Few Central Terms

Even an inquiry into the perception of people, such as the present one, requires the specification of the central terms used thereby indicating the way according to which their definitions were operationalized, together with the meanings attached to them for the purpose of this study. The most significant terms that need specification for the purpose of this study are the ones that have to do with different levels of *Khat* use and attachment to *Khat*. The rest of the terms used in the study are either self explanatory, explained in the text itself, or properly defined in Annex One, which deals with local terms.

Quite obviously, the task of defining those terms that concern differential use of and attachment to the *Khat*, is closely related to the highly contested issues of whether *Khat* is in the first place addictive or not and the kinds of mechanism by which its addictiveness operates. But, as this study is primarily a perception study that aims at unraveling the socioeconomic impacts and serving the search for viable policy responses, it has avoided being bogged down in such a contentious and futile

4

exercise[2]. It has instead worked on identifying and defining the different levels of *Khat* use and degrees of dependence on the basis of the own conception of people who use/abuse *Khat*. Thus it has identified and worked with the terms they use in various contexts to signify a person's degree of dependence, instead of imposing preconceived definitions siphoned from the literature on *Khat*. Needless to say, the meanings that people attach to the terms they frequently use in various circumstances are brought out from the texts of the in-depth interviews and group discussions held with them in the course of the data collection activities of the study.

In line with the above, what is derived from informants discourse on *Khat* is that the different terms signifying degrees of usage and attachment to *Khat* carry definitive meanings, although used rather liberally and are employed without specifying whether the user recognizes his/her degree of addiction. Thus, they represent definite gradings on a continuous scale or an unbroken continuum. They start with the highest degree of usage and attachment going down to the lowest, which people refer to as follows:

1. *Hambis* - In the Harar and the surrounding region in particular, one who is *"possessed"* or *"captured"* by *Khat;* a *Jäzba*, meaning one who chews morning, afternoon and night, does not think about work and neglects himself, and the welfare of others, etc.; in popular description, one who would not care as long as he gets more of *Khat*.

2. *Käbad Yä Č'at Suss / Käbad Yä Č'at Susse* or *Hailäña YäČ'at Suss / Hailäña Yä Č'at Susseña* - Heavy *Khat addiction* / heavy *Khat* addict.

3. *Yä Č'at Suss / Yä Č'at Susseña* - *Khat* addiction / *Khat* addict. Being *dependent on regular Khat consumption* without indication of the strength of the addiction.

---

[2] For instance, seven drug dependence categories produced by a group of WHO experts in 1956, are too general shed light on the degrees of *Khat* dependence that this study is concerned with, and are therefore of little use to it. The categories the experts identified are: (1) morphine type (2) barbiturate-alcohol type (3) cocaine type (4) cannabis type (5) amphetamine type (6) khat type, and (7) hallucinogen type. In his work on the use of *Khat* in North Yemen, John Kennedy who found this categorization unsatisfactory for his purpose instead used terms and concepts drawn from Yemen. Thus, he wrote of the usage of the relevant terms as follows: "In Yemeni usage, the word *mula'I* signifies one who is "tied to" qat; that is, dependent upon it, but rarely is one so designated regarded negatively. Another term *mut'wala*, used more in the Taiz region, also refers to dependence, but has a less strong implication. It more closely approximates our concept of "habituated". The term *mudman*, on the other hand, literally means "addicted," but it is generally reserved for either opium or alcohol dependence, and is rarely used in connection with quat" (Kennedy, 1987: 190-1).

4. *Yä Č'at Amäl* - *Khat* habit. Being in the habit of regular *Khat* consumption. A term denoting a lesser level of attachment as compared to *Yä Č'at Suss*.

5. *Bä Sine-srat Qami* - A person who chews *Khat* with discipline instead of abuse, with modesty in terms of place chosen, time allocated and amount consumed.

6. *Wäta-gäba Bay* - An "on-and-off" or infrequent *Khat* user. A person that is not yet habituated to, or dependent on *Khat*.

Hence, without further ado, by focusing on the English translations, which are given above, it is possible to get the sense of order in the level of use and attachment to *Khat* these various terms – heavy/strong addiction, addiction, dependence on / regular habit, modest/disciplined use, and "on-and-off"/ infrequent use – denote in this study.

1.3 Objectives of the Research

General objective

The overall objective of the study is to identify, assess and describe the current state and the socioeconomic impacts of *Khat* consumption and addiction, as well as attempts that are presently underway to reverse the trend with the ultimate aim of informing national level policy formulation and intervention.

Specific objectives

In line with the above, the specific objectives of the study are the following:

1. Identify, assess, compare and describe *Khat* related situations in Harar and Assosa Cities concerning:

   - Introduction, pathways, prevalence, patterns trends of *Khat* consumption and addiction

   - Socioeconomic impacts of *Khat* consumption addiction at the following levels:
     o Family life and household economy
     o Gender
     o Children
     o Local economy and local community

- o Health
- o Education
- o Crime and juvenile delinquency
- o Civil service delivery and civil servants

2. Identify and assess the measures undertaken by governmental and non-governmental agents to counteract the spread of *Khat* consumption and addiction and/or to rehabilitate addicts in Assosa and Harar Cities.

3. Assess the existence and levels of implementation of *Khat* related policies, laws and regulations at the national and regional levels.

4. Identify realistic alternative pathways for policy formulation/reform to hinder the spread of *Khat* consumption and addiction at the national level.

1.4   Research Sites

As this comparative case study of the socioeconomic impacts of *Khat* addiction in Harar and Assosa cities is part of a larger partnership engagement, its field site selection was a predetermined affair. Thus, the main body of empirical data informing the study was collected through field research conducted in the two cities. However, some additional information was obtained from few sites outside the City of Assosa, namely, Tongo, Kurmuk and Bambassi Towns, where the partner NGOs themselves or their associates have some ongoing activities relevant to the study. Moreover, national level supplementary information was also obtained from relevant institutions and persons through a limited data collection activity in Addis Ababa.

1.5   Method

1.5.1   Approach

A. The study collected both *qualitative* and *quantitative* data. While its main focus was the collection and analysis of qualitative data, attempts were made to obtain and incorporate quantitative data generated through estimates of FGD/I participants and also those that could be skimmed from archives, government reports and published and unpublished research manuscripts.

B. To a certain extent, the study was guided by the principles of *action research*, in that two partner NGOs that were engaged in activities directed at reversing the spread of *Khat* consumption and at rehabilitating addicts at the time of the study, were involved in some of the stages of the study –particularly, in the finalization of the study design, identification and tracing of informants, and the validation of its findings.

1.5.2 Methods of data collection and analysis

The research involved the collection and analysis of primary and secondary data through intensive fieldwork conducted at the two sites, and an additional limited scale fieldwork in Addis Ababa. Furthermore, the study benefited from whatever secondary information that was available regarding the socioeconomic impacts of *Khat* consumption and addiction in the two sites in particular and the country in general.

The main primary data collection methods employed, were:

- **In-depth interview** with key informants that are listed in Table 1 on the page that follows. The in-depth interviews covered, but were not limited to, issues such as personal and family histories as well as recollections regarding community-wide events as they relate to *Khat*.

- **Focus-group-discussion/interview** with groups listed in Table 1 on the page that follows. The focus-group-discussions/interviews focused on, but were not limited to, issues such as historical developments and timelines, old and current patterns, emerging trends, and general prevalence (such as site specific estimates of consumption and expenditure.)

- **Observation:** In the course of the fieldwork informing the field team made both intended/planned and unintended/opportunistic observation of the *Khat* markets, chewing dens, the condition of the *Khat* consumers/addicts, the rehabilitation facilities and activities, and events such as the graduation ceremonies of rehabilitated addicts, etc.

- In addition to the above, attempts were made -- though with limited success -- to obtain **quantitative and qualitative secondary data** relevant to the study that could be analyzed/reanalyzed together with the study's own primary data. The two major sources of the secondary data were:

  ❖ Official records obtained from various governmental and non-governmental organizations (such as CSA, Federal Ministries, FMHACA, Regional Bureaus and courts, as well as hospitals in the study areas), and

8

❖ Published material on the socioeconomic and health impacts of *Khat* consumption and addiction in general, and those on Ethiopia in particular.

1.5.3 Issues, data sources and data collection methods

The following matrix makes a systematic joint presentation of the issues on which information was sought (derived from the specific objectives of the research given above) together with the sources from which information was obtained and the data collection methods employed. This matrix was followed, albeit with a margin of flexibility, as the roadmap that guided the study guaranteeing full control over the data collection process as well as the assignment of the material thus collected into the various sections of the study's report.

Table 2: Matrix of Themes, Data Sources and Data Collection Methods

Theme	Data Source	Method
Origin, & prevalence, trends, patterns, and factors behind the spread of *Khat* consumption and addiction	Library/Archives/Internet	Literature Review
	Elders and community leaders	FGD/I
	Khat traders/providers	FGD/I
	Addicts, ex-addicts, and addicts in rehab	KII/FGD/I
	BoLSA, BoWCYA, BoE, BoH, University and Court officials, police officers and health workers	KII/ FGD/I
Socioeconomic Impacts of *Khat* consumption and addition	Library/Archives/Internet	Literature Review
	Addicts, ex-addicts/addicts in rehab	KII/FGD/I
	Family of addicts, addicts in rehab/ sex workers	KII/FGD/I
	Religious leaders and community elders	KII/FGD/I
	BoLSA, BoWCYA, BoE, BoH, Univ. and Court officials, police officers and health workers	KII/FGD/I
Attempts at controlling *Khat* consumption and addiction, and the way forward in terms of policy and intervention	Library/Archives/Internet	Literature Review
	Addicts, ex-addicts/addicts in rehab	KII/FGD/I
	Wives &family of addicts and addicts in rehab	KII/FGD/I
	Religious leaders and community elders	KII/FGD/I
	BoLSA, BoWCYA, BoE, BoH, University and Court officials, police officers and health workers	KII/FGD/I
	MoLSA and FMHACA officials, mental health professionals, Dangerous Drugs Circulation Control Div.	KII

Table 2, below, summarizes the fieldwork activity informing the study that was actually undertaken in terms of the methods used, and the sources of information together with their numbers.

Table 3: Summary of Data Collection Methods, Sources of Information and their Numbers

	Method of Data Collection and Sources of Information	No.
1	In-depth interview with addicts (+observation)	6
2	In-depth interview with addicts in rehab and ex-addicts (+observation)	9
3	In-depth interview with family members of addicts, addicts in rehab, and ex-addicts	5
4	In-depth interview with sex-workers (+observation)	5
5	In-depth interview with mental health workers (+observation)	3
6	In-depth interview with growers, traders, etc	2
7	FGD with religious leaders and elders	4
8	FGD and in-depth interview with university officials and student representatives	3
9	FGD/I and in-depth interview with regional bureau and city admin officials	4
10	FGD/I and in-depth interview with court officials and police officers	2
11	FGD/I and in-depth interview with representatives of CSOs working on *Khat*	6
12	Interview with or brief communication from federal-level officials	5

1.6   Data Collection Fieldwork

The empirical data informing the study were collected in the course of five fieldwork trips made to the research sites. Three trips, of three to 10 days duration each, were made to Assosa, of which the first was to conduct exploratory research, the second to undertake data collection proper (22 - 31 August 20150, and the third to validate the data and take care of certain loose ends. Similarly, data collection in Harar was undertaken through an exploratory field trip of three days preceding the main fieldwork that lasted for 9 days (2 - 10 September 2015).

Data Collection in Assosa, Harar and Addis Ababa were undertaken being guided, but not always strictly followed, by checklists addressed to the various categories of informants. The checklists were prepared on the basis of information siphoned in the course of the reviewing of literature on *Khat* and the exploratory trips, both of which preceded the data collection fieldwork. The b) that were employed are those for: (a) Elders, and Community & Religious Leaders' FGD (b) Civil Society Organizations' FGD (c) Addicts', Ex-addicts' and Addicts' in Rehab KII (c) Addicts', Ex-addicts' and Addicts in Rehab Family Members' KII (e) Government and university Officials' FGD and KII. Other categories of informants such as sex-workers and individuals that were found to be exceptionally informative were interviewed freely, i.e., without recourse to a checklist.

1.7   Scope and Policy Implication

1. **Scope**: The study has generated information aiming at a better understanding of the causes, patterns, trends, and above all the socioeconomic impacts of *Khat* consumption and addiction at various levels, in the cities of Harar and Assosa. The study was limited to collecting and analyzing relevant data focusing on the two cities and their immediate vicinities. Thus, the focus of the study was the identification, sketching, and understanding of patterns, trends and impacts rather than measuring such magnitudes as the quantity of *Khat* that is consumed, the exact numbers of addicts and secondary victims, or the amounts of its various impacts.

2. **Policy Implication:** It ought to be noted, also, that while the findings of this case study of two cities essentially refers to the situations in the two urban centers from which the data were collected, they are in general terms pertinent to other communities throughout the country. Hence, the relevance of the study's findings in informing national level policy reform and improved intervention cannot be questioned on the basis of its limited case study nature.

1.8   Reporting and Validation

Upon completion of the study, its findings were reported to the FSS in a draft form, and discussed at a national conference of researchers, staff of the two partner NGOs, representative of relevant government ministries, and agencies such as MoH, MoLSA, MoFEC, FMHACA, Dangerous Drugs Circulation Control Division of the Federal Police, as well as members of the medical, social work and legal professions, and members of the donor and civil society communities with interest in the issue of substance use/abuse in general and that of *Khat* in particular. Thus, this publication has benefited from inputs provided through this validation conference.

2 Escalating Consumption/Addiction and Socioeconomic Impacts of *Khat*, and Attempts at addressing them in Assosa

In order to better understand and appreciate the past and current state of the prevalence, as well as the socioeconomic impacts of *Khat* in Assosa City, it would be necessary to provide a brief picture of the general infrastructural and economic development situation, and the demographic profile of the Regional State.

Founded around the beginning of the 20th Century and having remained a provincial administrative center of secondary importance for most of its life, Assosa City is now the capital of Benishangul-Gumuz National Regional State, which is one of the ethnic-based regions constituting the Ethiopian federal state. The region and its capital acceded to their current eminence only after the regime change in 1991. Before that, the zones that now constitute the regional state were the remote and neglected "backwoods" of Gojjam and Wolega Administrative Regions. For this reason, Benishangul-Gumuz -- together with Afar and Somali NRS -- is usually referred to as an "emerging" regional state to indicate its lagging behind the rest of the country in terms of economic development. The region faced major challenges to economic development, due to lack of transportation and communications infrastructure. Until a major road that connects the Metekel Zone and the Asosa Zone together with a bridge over the Abbay (Blue Nile) River was built in 2012, one had to travel through Wollega and Gojjam in the neighboring regional states of Oromia and Amhara, a distance of 1,250 kilometers that it is now cut to around 378 kilometers. Still, conditions for travel within zones are generally poor and subject to disruption during the rainy season. Further developments, particularly expansion of electric power supply, mobile telephone connectivity, health and educational facilities, as well as the establishment of a university and an international airport at Assosa City, the ongoing construction of the Grand Ethiopian Renaissance Dam (GERD), and the proliferating commercial farms -- of which much has been said by way of "land grabbing" -- are heralding the promise of change.

Benishangul-Gumuz Regional State has a total population of 784,345, with urban inhabitants numbering 105,926 or 13.51% of the population. It has an estimated area of 49,289.46 square kilometres, with a density of 15.91 people per square kilometre. Ethnic wise, the population of the region includes the Berta (25.90%), Amhara (21.25 %), Gumuz (21.11%), Oromo (13.32%), Shinasha (7.59%), Agaw-Awi (4.24%) and

Mao (1.90) (CSA 2008: 96). Concerning religion, 45.4% of the population were Moslem, 33.0% were Orthodox Christians, 13.3% were Protestant, and 7.1% followed traditional beliefs (CSA 2008: 112).

The ethnic distribution of the urban population, which is at variance from that of the total population of the region -- and important for the purpose of this study -- was as follows in 2007. Ethnically, the urban population was distributed among Amhara (37.42%), Oromo (22.14%), Gumuz (10.20%), Berta (8.98%), Shinasha (7.80%), Agaw-Awi (5.92%) and Mao (1.66). Thus, the ethnic groups exogenous to the region preponderate among urban inhabitants, with the Amhara and the Oromo, taken together, accounting for a clear majority (59.56%) of the urban population (CSA, 2008: 96). Likewise, the religious distribution of the urban population, too, is decidedly skewed towards the beliefs associated with the exogenous ethnic groups. Thus, 51.2% of the urban inhabitants were Orthodox Christians, 29.1% of the Moslem, 18.3% Protestant, and only 0.6% professed various traditional beliefs (CSA 2008: 112). Considering the very limited level of urbanization in the Regional State, and the primacy of Assosa City among the few urban centres in the Region, it can be safely surmised that the ethnic and religious distributions presented in this paragraph about urban Benishangul-Gumuz very closely reflect the situation prevalent in Assosa City.

2.1 Introduction into, Spread and Prevalence of *Khat* Consumption and Addiction in Assosa

2.1.1 Introduction into and spread of *Khat* in Assosa

In Assosa, *Khat* consumption and addiction are of relative recent origin. The phenomenon was virtually unknown in the whole of Benishangul-Gumuz until the 1970s. In the late-70s *Khat* began to be consumed in Mao-Komo and Bambassi *Wäräda* following the footsteps of migrants from other parts of the country. Yet, up till the 1990s, only a few people working in the modern sector such as teachers, civil servants, drivers, and the like consumed *Khat*. It was as of 1997, and particularly since the year 2000, that both its production and consumption spread in and around Assosa, with large numbers of youngsters beginning to emulate the actions of those people whom they considered to be modern or educated. Particularly, in the wake of the administrative decentralization that devolved significant role and authority to the Region and the *Wäräda*, *Khat* consumption, which was limited to Assosa, spread to areas such as Menghie, Kurmuk, and Gizen. This was further facilitated by expansion of the road network, which facilitated the regular and timely delivery of *Khat* to various parts of the Region. Thus, ever since that time *Khat* became a dominant stimulant in Benishangul-Gumuz in general and Assosa in particular; and in this sense, it speedy spread can be considered a *developmental hazard*, i.e., unintended deleterious outcome of developmental processes.

In the course of the FGD with representatives of civil society organizations working on *Khat* (CS-FGD), the leadership of BGDAN was forthcoming regarding the origin and spread of *Khat* in Benishangul-Gumuz in general and Assosa in particular. At the very beginning of its project, BGDAN conducted an exploratory study on the origins of *Khat* in the Region. The results show that the practice of chewing *Khat* started in the 1970s, around Mao-Komo with Islamic religious leaders, who used it to help them keep awake during prayer vigils. Sometimes, it was given to women (BGDAN, Baseline Survey, undated). Tea made from it, known as *Hawza*, was given to children also. In Bambassi, it was members of the first wave of spontaneous settlers that brought the habit along with them from Wollo. But, with the expansion of developmental activities in the region around the turn of the Millennium and ever since it has spread through the ranks of those working in the modern sector, and through them to the youth.

The same study by BGDAN revealed that the production of *Khat* has now expanded to almost all *Wäräda*, including those *Wäräda* inhabited by the Berta, where it was not known at all. *Khat* production seems to have expanded from the neighboring *Wäräda* of Oromia, as well. In Mao-Komo, farmers have started to replace their coffee trees with *Khat* plants as of the year 2000. The Welfare Monitoring Survey has confirmed that nearly a fifth (19.25%) of houselhold in the Region owned *Khat* plants in 2011 (CSA. 2012b: Table 9.1, b).

According to one of the participants of the CS-FGD, the indigenous people in Mao-Komo used to chew *Khat* without abuse of any other substances, but with the coming of Sudanese refugees, *Shisha* smoking was introduced into the area. Furthermore, other newcomers (civil servants, etc) have also brought along with them the habit of smoking cigarettes and that of the drinking alcohol into the area, further compounding the problem of *Khat* dependence and addiction.

The recentness of the spread of *Khat* consumption in the Region was attested by nearly all of the in-depth informants of the study as well. Ato Melkamu Tadesse (Deputy Head of the Education Bureau) maintained that the spread of *Khat* in the different parts the Region is a recent phenomenon that gathered momentum around the year 2000.

Ato Befekadu Gebremeskel (Elder, Retired Teacher) describe the process of which he is a witness as follows:

> *Khat* was unknown in the Region in the old days. I recall how only two people, both of them university students who came to the Assosa in 1969 on their National Service [a one year mandatory service for all would-be university graduates at the time] chewed *Khat* and this caused negative reaction from the local community that considered the practice immoral. Before the spread of *Khat*, Beghi was known for high production of cereals, but know *Khat* has taken over most of the land there. The wide spread of *Khat* use in the Region began around 1989, with visible consequences on students' performance and crime. As of 1997, *Khat* came to reign over Assosa (ጫት በአሶሳ ነገሰ).

2.1.2 Patterns and Prevalence of *Khat* Consumption and Addiction in Assosa

In the opinion of the study's informants, most of the male adults in present-day Assosa City chew *Khat,* and the practice has also spread to almost all *Wäräda* of Benishangul-Gumuz. Its consumption is more widespread among those employed in the modern sector including teachers, students, and civil servants. While smoking is equally common, alcohol is not widely consumed, as the majority of the city's residents are Moslems.[3]

The BGDAN study has found that an average of 15 *Jämbie* (about 22.5 Quintal) of *Khat* are received by the city every day in addition to whatever is produced within the city's limits. However, not all that is brought in from other areas is consumed in the City. About two-thirds of that which comes in from outside are sent out to other outlaying *Wäräda* of the Region (BGDAN, Baseline Survey, undated: 7).

Pushed by the growing demand for it, *Khat* production has made headway into most of the *Wäräda* of the Region. Its consumption has now spread to almost all *Wäräda* of the Region, and its production has followed this to many *Wäräda*, including to those where it was almost totally unknown. Currently, farmers have started to replace their coffee plantation with that of *Khat*, particularly in Mao-Komo *Wäräda*.

---

[3] According to the 2007 Census, nearly three-quarters of the Town's population (74.08%) were Moslem (CSA, 2007).

Khat marketing, too, has become so widespread and important to the city's economy, that the city administration has assigned a market place in the middle of the city dedicated solely to it. The market place is the hub of *Khat* related activities involving a large number of traders, middlemen, children and young-adult peddlers of all sorts of *Khat*-associated materials such as plastic bags, bottled water and chewing gums, as well as truck drivers and transporters.

Ye-nege Tesfa MSE-FGD (Tongo Town, Mao-Komo *Wärädä*): the three young men in the group reported that they used to chew *Khat* for whole days, and every day. They added that they were able to easily support their very high consumption as *Khat* is produced abundantly in the *Wärädä* and is therefore quite cheap.

In Assosa, *Khat* is chewed at all times of the day and in almost all places, be they public or private. However, typically, it is chewed in *Khat bet*. Tobacco and *Shisha* smoking, as well as that of cannabis accompany its consumption. Alcohol is the primary choice of *Č'äbsi* for all, save the Moslem population.

The BGDAN study has revealed the following concerning the types and order of importance of *Khat* consumption places:

> As for chewing place, three major categories are observable. The first one is the one provided by a category of commercial sex workers. That is, there are commercial sex workers who earn their living by providing chewing room and other substances – mostly *Shisha* – to smoke. After chewing chat and smoking *Shisha*, there is also a possibility of having sex with the [waitresses]. The second is in the private house/room: the necessary ceremony is arranged in the house and chewing takes place with colleagues or alone. The last is in public places: in [hotel] rooms and outdoors of hotels, in cafeterias, in DSTV [show] rooms, in shops, etc., (BGDAN, Baseline Survey, undated: 6-7).

2.1.3 Factors behind the escalating *Khat* Consumption and Addiction in Assosa

Informants identified some ten factors, which are mostly bi-products of the speedy and positive socioeconomic development that the country in general and the Region in particular are experiencing, as being behind *Khat* consumption and addiction. The factors they identified are listed below without any order of importance:

1. Expansion of government services, including the various extension services, and the concomitant swelling of the ranks of civil servants

2. Decentralization, particularly devolution of administrative authority to the Region and the *Wäräda* that has spread out civil servants far and wide

3. Expansion public works activities that has brought large numbers of engineers, technicians, and skilled and unskilled construction workers into the area

4. Expansion of the road network, which facilitated the regular and timely delivery of fresh *Khat* at lower prices

5. Expansion of education, and the resultant inward movement of teachers and students with *Khat* and related substance habits

6. Youngsters' tendency to emulate *Khat* consuming persons they considered to be modern or educated, including teachers

7. In-migration of re-settlers from Wollo and refugees from Sudan

8. Easy accessibility and affordability of *Khat* in the city

9. Absence of places of healthy entertainment, particularly for the youth, and

10. Finally, lack of regulation and control.

The spread of *Khat* consumption and addiction is further fueled by certain misconceptions regarding its supposed health benefits. Abba Yohannes (Administrator of Medhnialem Church, Assosa *Hagäräsebkät* of the Ethiopian Tewahedo Orthodox Church (ETOC) pointed out that certain people get into the habit of chewing the substance in the erroneous belief that it possesses the quality of reducing blood pressure, and the like.

Informants were unanimous in pointing out that substance abuse is incremental. Many regular chewers start with *Khat*, and proceed to smoking tobacco, drinking alcoholic beverages, and end up in using other hard drugs. Informants also link this stepwise spread of addiction to the influence of immigrants. One of the participants of the CS-FGD maintained that indigenous people of Mao-Komo used to chew *Khat* without abuse of any other substances, but with the coming of Sudanese refugees, *Shisha* smoking was introduced into the area. Furthermore, other newcomers (civil servants, teachers, drivers, etc) have also brought along with them the habits of smoking cigarettes and that of the drinking alcohol into the area.

Ato Melkamu, Deputy Head of the Education Bureau, said, he believes that,

Khat spreads to students from teachers who often send them to buy/fetch *Khat*. In addition, *Khat* chewing people such as contractors and drivers serve as negative role models for the youth. *Khat* also spreads as a result of migration as when youth from Beghi where it is quite commonly chewed come to Assosa to attend school, they help introduce the habit to other youth. Investment, resettlement, and trade have helped to spread *Khat* chewing in Assosa.

2.2   Socioeconomic impacts of *Khat* consumption and addiction in Assosa

The study has looked into the socioeconomic impacts of *Khat* consumption and addiction in Assosa City at the following levels: family life and household economy, women and children, local economy and local community, health, education, crime and its correction, and civil service delivery.

2.2.1   Family life and household economy

In Assosa, *Khat* addicts and heavy users often access their *Khat* supply through a vicious cycle of credit, credit payment, and back to credit, supplemented by cash-on-hand purchase with borrowed money that is followed by the uphill struggle to settle that debt, thereby ruining their household economy and shaming their family. Those who are almost always under pressure by their many creditors and debtors, are forced to hide, lie, and then fight with their spouses, get emotionally disturbed, and ultimately quit or are dismissed from their jobs. Families of *Khat* addicts often engrossed by financial burden as they have to foot the health bill of these addicts who suffer from physical and mental ill health. Domestic theft is also reported as being common among *Khat* addicts and heavy users leading to dissention within the family. Domestic disagreements and fights between spouses, disputes between parents and their children as well as among siblings, all on account of *Khat* is common. Information garnered in the course of the fieldwork has ascertained that quarreling with parents on various pretexts has become more common among young people following the spread of the habit of chewing *Khat*.

As attested by virtually all of the informants of the study, the heavy use and addiction to *Khat* of husbands is contributing towards marital discord that ultimately leads to divorce and family dissolution through the neglect of the welfare of wives and the failure of husbands to fulfill their manly duty due to impotence, accumulating over time.

According to the CS-FGD, since families that are plagued with *Khat* fail to engage in community-wide activities such as visiting the sick, attending weddings and burials, and the like, inter-family ties and solidarity is gradually weakening.

A participant of the Anti-Corruption Commission & Police Commission-FGD, Deputy Inspector Hagos Yeshak noted that the Police often receive complaints concerning domestic disturbance and fights that are all common among *Khat* addicts.

2.2.2 Women and children

Women are impacted more by the *Khat*-chewing habits of their husbands than the other way round, as they are the ones responsible for managing their households' economy and making ends meet at all costs. They suffer being the subject of domestic violence of all sorts. Their heavy user or addict husbands ignore them both emotionally and sexually. Many marriages are challenged and often dissolved on account of impotence that follows on the heavy use of *Khat*, according to a virtual totality of our informants.

Addict or heavy user parents, who are not in control of themselves, ignore the welfare of children. They directly or indirectly encouraged their children to develop the habit; and many children are forced to engage as delivery-workers and as peddlers of all sorts of *Khat* attendant materials at the *Khat* market, to the detriment of their education. Through such close association with the substance and its users, they are then gradually promoted to the status of regular users and addicts. Children are orphaned or abandoned on account of rampant divorce by their *Khat* dependent parents and the subsequent family dissolution. Children, who are both physically and mentally tender and vulnerable, suffer the brunt of domestic conflict and the subsequent sufferings of the parents they naturally love and care for

Wz. Nefissa Mussa, Head of the Children, the Office of Women, Children and Youth Affairs (OoCWYA) of Kurmuk *Wäräda* observed:

> Many youths in our *Wäräda* are addicted to *Khat*. *Khat* addiction is also widespread among women who have migrated to the *Wäräda* in search of work. It has also spread to the rural areas in the *Wäräda*, where youngsters as well as older people now chew *Khat*.

> Economic deprivation and other adverse impacts on the wellbeing of wives due to *Khat* addiction of their husbands are common. As a result of this, our efforts to bring about economic empowerment of women by

engaging them in income generation activities are not successful. Economic hardships on the households, inability to properly raise children, and divorce are the major consequences of *Khat* addiction in the *Wäräda*.

Wz. Freheiwot Abebe Gobena, Deputy Head of Benishangul-Gumuz NRS BoWCYA added:

> The office works to improve the social, political, and economic participation of women and the youth. However, addiction of people, particularly to *Khat*, has made achieving this goal difficult. This is particularly true of young men who fail to participate in the opportunities created for them because of their addiction to *Khat*. The problem is so serious in Assosa that when discussion was held on GTP II, many of the participants asked how the plan could be successfully implemented while most of the productive labor force is shackled to *Khat*.

> Women do not normally chew *Khat* in this area, but they are still affected by it in many ways. *Khat* consumption by men negatively impacts their wives and marriage. One of these is the sexual incapacity it engenders on men, which is widely spoken of as a cause for the dissatisfaction of wives leading to divorce.

> Children are involved in the *Khat* chewing business from their tender age, as they are required to run errands in purchasing *Khat* and related materials for grown-ups. This gradually leads children to grow into *Khat* consumers. I have heard the story of a small boy who used to be sent to purchase *Khat* asked the question: "Is there no *Khat* for small boys as well" (ሁልጊዜ ጫት ተራ የሚላክ አንድ ትንሽ ልጅ "የልጅ ጫት የለም ወይ ብሎ ጠየቀ" ሲባል ሰምቻለሁ). Who will inherit the country under such circumstances? Is it people or money that is more important?

> The youth are turned away from productive life by *Khat*, since it makes them live in a dream world of enrichment without work. The absence of places of healthy entertainment is another factor that pushes the young towards *Khat*.

Wz. Tsigie Tarekegne, Youth, Participation and Empowerment Core Process Owner in the BoWCYA added:

> What my fellow FGD participants have said about the impact of *Khat* on the sexual life of married couples is a well-known fact. It is common

knowledge that *Khat* chewing reduces the sexual performance of men, but people don't talk about it openly. It is often the cause of disagreement with their wives.

Moreover, when a parent chews *Khat*, he neglects childcare, thus children of *Khat* chewers get no follow up from parents, are not sent to school, and drop out of school more often. In addition, *Khat*-chewing men spend much money on *Khat* and alcohol for *Č'äbsi*.

I ought to stress the role of educated people in popularizing *Khat* abuse in the Region. Many *Khat* chewers (such as teachers, civil servants) send young boys to *Khat* markets to buy *Khat* for them. This exposes the boys to the habit.

In the course of the FGD with religious leaders and elders, Ato Abebaw Sissay (a retired school support staff) told the sad story of what has happened to his son who passed his school leaving examination and joined Arba Minch University. Unfortunately, once the son was there, he got addicted to *Khat* chewing and cigarette smoking, and has returned home and remained under treatment for mental illness since 1998. The father expressed his bitterness by saying, "our children are enslaved by *Khat* addiction. The reason for having a government/state was so as it would rule over us with order!" (ልጆቻችን የሱስ ባሪያዎች ሆነዋል፡፡ መንግስት የኖረን በስርአት አንዲገዛን ነበር እኮ፡፡)

There is one additional trajectory through which *Khat* affects the situation of a category of women, the number of which, although indeterminate, is known to be very high in Ethiopia. That is the group of sex-workers. It an established truth that stimulants and drugs, illicit or otherwise, are intrinsically linked to the recruitment or the slipping of young girls into prostitution. The abuse of alcohol and drugs is in fact an integral aspect of prostitution. For instance, a survey conducted on prostitutes in Melbourne, Australia found that 87% of female and 65% of male prostitutes covered had used drugs other than alcohol and tobacco in the last year preceding it. (Norma Marshall and Jane Hendtlass, 1986:1). Prostitution is so tightly intertwined with drug abuse to defy attempt at differentiating the cause from the effect among them. It is even difficult to tell which one of them opens the way and which one follows.

Informants of the study, the sex-workers in particular, were clear regarding the important place *Khat* holds in their lives as sex-workers. They told the field team that *Khat* was crucial in making their lives as sex-workers bearable. They said that it helps them to stay awake long into the night waiting for clients, entertaining and trapping them, and performing their sometimes-painful duties. Since the facilitation of the sale of alcoholic drink by helping themselves to as much as possible to it is part of their job descriptions and terms of employment by the bar owners, alcohol further tightens the belt by which they are attached to *Khat* as drinking alcohol for *Č'äbsi* is a must for their clients as well as themselves. Furthermore, the sex-worker informants of the study, were open in admitting their addiction status saying that they regularly spend their income from sex-work on the purchase of *Khat* which they chew in groups whiling away their boring leisure time during the day. They also invariably added that they would not be able to quit chewing *Khat* unless they at the same time get out of sex-work and distance themselves from waitress work at the bars where alcoholic drinks are sold and drunk in abundance.

2.2.3   Local economy and local community

The fact that this study being on Assosa City, this section, too, focuses on the city's economy and those of the communities within it.

The direct financial contribution of *Khat* to the city's revenue is not significant, and negative when weighed together with its costs, according to informants working in the sector. This is because of the existence of as many illegal traders in the city that are mobile and hard to control.

Obviously, *Khat* has indirect contribution to the local economy by facilitating other business as well. But, its social and economic costs far outweigh this benefit. Let alone its indirect well-known social and economic costs, its direct adverse impact on the local economy in robbing it of the productive labor of its young, cannot be overstated.

Ato Abebe Senbeta, Social Rehabilitation and Resource Mobilization Officer at BoLSA elucidate the above point saying, "a casual worker earns 70–80 Birr per day in Assosa, but our young men instead of seizing the opportunity and improving their livelihoods, spend their time chewing *Khat* for whole days".

According to BGDAN's baseline study, while the law imposes a 100% sales tax on *Khat*, this is not properly enforced in Assosa. The *Khat* traders are expected to pay only 15% profit tax plus 10 Birr per *Jämbie*[4]. But, even the 15% profit tax is collected

---

[4] A load or stack (Amharic *Shäkem*) of about 1.5 Quintal used in *Khat* wholesale trading in Assosa.

from only one-third of the traders in city. The remaining two-thirds are not licensed and operate from the shops of the legally licensed ones, and thereby easily avoid making their share of contribution to the city's economy. Thus, the revenue generated from *Khat* trading in the whole of Assosa *Wärädä* as a whole (*sic*) is within the range of 300,000 to 400,000 Birr per year, and way below the marketing and consumption that goes on.

Ato Tesfaye Nemera, Assosa City Revenue Office, Revenue Collection Process Owner, described the mechanics and the level of *Khat's* contribution to the city's revenue as follows:

> The law provides that tax on *Khat* should be based by weight, but there are no scales at the check-posts. Last year, 60,000 Birr was collected as check-post tax (የኬላ ቀረጥ). Thus, the total annual tax revenue of the city (*sic*) from *Khat* doesn't exceed 100,000 Birr; and this limited financial benefit must also be weighed against the social costs of *Khat* to the city.

> We are now trying to implement VAT following lessons learnt from Hawassa and other cities. But this may be difficult since the total sales of *Khat* traders here is not higher than 500,000 Birr per annum, and imposing VAT on them would therefore be in violation of the proclamation on VAT.

> There are 45 legally registered *Khat* traders in the city, but also as many, if not many more, illegal ones who are mobile and hard to control. The latter are different from those in the East of the Country in that their capital being very low, while not as powerful they are quite slippery.

> *Shisha bet*, where *Khat* is chewed and *Shisha* is smoked, are common in the city. Although these are not licensed and therefore illegal, it is difficult to control them. This is because the police officers that are expected to close them are in league with their owners. Thus, they get information about any impending search campaign ahead of it and simply melt away hiding their equipments.

2.2.4　Health and health service

Informants in Assosa were unanimous that *Khat* is seriously impacting the health status of a large section of its heavy user and addict population. The findings on the subject are categorized and presented under the three headings of physical, mental, and reproductive health.

Physical health: Most addicts, ex-addicts, and addicts under rehabilitation report constipation, stomach ulcer, emaciation, skin-disease, etc. as the major physical ailments afflicting heavy or long-time *Khat* users.

Mental health: Psychiatric health workers, as well as ex-addicts and addicts in rehab cite forgetfulness, moodiness, hallucination, depression, and psychosis as the common mental health problems that are caused or amplified by heavy and long-time *Khat* use. One ex-addict FGD participant said that, he used to behave like "an unshackled mad man whenever he experienced *Dukak*".

Reproductive health: Ex-addicts, wives and sex-workers report very low concern for sex and inability to perform by men who chew *Khat*. A group of young ex-addicts that are organized in an MSE explained this as follows: They said that even when they desired sex, they suffered from erectile dysfunction. One of them expressed his experience by saying "I sometimes felt the urge to have sex, but when I tried to do it, the meter read 'battery low!'" (See Box #3 for more).

Regarding the linkages between *Khat* consumption and sexual life, all CS-FGD participants held the opinion that chewing *Khat* reduces a person's sexual drive and causes erectile dysfunction. Even if and when one has the desire to have sex after chewing *Khat*, he would not be able to engage in sex, unless he consume a large amount of alcohol to counteract the effects of the consumed *Khat*.

Abba Yohannes, Administrator of Medhanealem Church, Assosa *Hagäräsebkät* of ETOC, was of the opinion that there are misconceptions about *Khat*, with some people believing that its helps reduce blood pressure, and the like, while *Khat* has only detrimental physical and psychological impacts including depression and impotence.

Box 1:*Khat* and Sexual Life: From the Perspective of Two Sex-workers on

23-year-old NS, sex worker since 2 years ago, reported that she chews *Khat* to help her stay awake during her long working nights, and also help her drink more of the beer that is offered to her by potential clients, which is her duty to do per her employment agreement with the owner of the establishment. Chewing *Khat* makes her inactive, both sexually and socially. She spends about 50 Birr per day on *Khat*, and recognizes that *Khat* is harmful. Her customers that are high on *Khat* have difficulty in attaining erection, and keep on asking her to keep on trying in helping them to achieve it. She says, most of the time this becomes impossible, as, in her own words, "there is nothing there, it is only...!" (ምንም የለም እኮ፤ ... ብቻ ነው!)Therefore, she is forced to renegotiate the deal giving back to the unhappy customer half of what he had paid upfront and keeping the remainder for herself as compensation for her unsuccessful labors. She plans to stop chewing *Khat* along with leaving the sex profession.

22 year-old SN, sex worker since 3 years ago, said: She chews *Khat* during the day to overcome boredom. She drinks more if she chews *Khat*. She doesn't feel much difference regarding her sexual drive and performance due to *Khat* chewing, but most of her customers that have chewed *Khat* can't achieve erection unless they drink alcohol, which again has its own negative consequences on sex. She says she can't and won't stop chewing *Khat* unless she stops commercial sex-work.

During the FGD with Yenege Tesfa MSE members, the three young men in the group reported that they used to chew *Khat* the whole day, every day. They stated that they had very low sexual activity when chewing *Khat*. They had little desire for sex, and didn't perform well, when they got the opportunity.

Box 2: *Khat* and the Family Lives of Selam Atkiltena Ferafrie Jimla Negd Maheber Members' (Bambassi)

All six members were, by their own frank admission, *Khat* addicts. Two of them reported that they have now fully stopped chewing *Khat*, while the rest said that they have reduced their consumption. In addition, those who chew *Khat* now stated that they no longer drink alcohol.

The FGD participants listed some of the deleterious effect that *Khat* had on their lives, including increased spending, forgetfulness, moodiness, hallucinations, and impotence. One of the FGD participant said that, he used to behave like "an unshackled mad man when under *Khat Dukak*".

All of them stress the negative impact of *Khat* on sexual desire. They would go home late at night and turn their backs towards their wives as they lay down, making their wives suspicious of extra-marital affairs, which they readily denied. Even when they desired sex, they would suffer from erectile dysfunction, they said. One of them humorously expressed his experience as follows: "I sometimes felt the urge to have sex, but when I tried to perform, the meter read 'battery low!'" These young men were adamant in affirming that, thanks to *Khat*, there was no much activity in their bedrooms in spite of them being at the prime of their youth

A third member of the FGD related his story as follow, "I used to spend up to 80 Birr per day on *Khat*, I didn't wash my cloths, and if I happened to see or imagine of *Khat* while I was sitting in class, I used to jump out through the classroom window and leave school. I was married for a while, but my wife left me because she felt that I was married to *Khat* rather than to her".

At this point, it would be necessary to have a brief look at the findings of medical science on the effect of *Khat* on human health in general and on reproductive health in particular, in order to compare them to what has been learnt from this study's informants on the subject. The scientific literature overwhelmingly testifies that *Khat* chewing is behind a number of human ill health. While many writers on the subject, consider scientific research on the *chemical connections* between *Khat* abuse and its impact in terms of dependency, mental health conditions, sexual performance, and the like, remains inconclusive, calling for further in-depth research into the exact mechanisms by which the ingredients of *Khat* lead to various physical and mental illnesses, almost all of them affirm its adverse impacts on human health. Thus, the overcautious stance of writers regarding the inconclusiveness of scientific research on the 'chemical connection' between *Khat* chewing and health hazards cannot be justifiably used as a ground for rejecting the linkage totally.

The international as well as the Ethiopian scientific literature are also in agreement concerning the adverse impact of *Khat* on human reproductive health. A study by Mwenda *et al*, 2003, which retrieved and analyzed relevant articles and abstracts cited in international journals from 1961 to 2002, arrived at the following data synthesis:

> Analysis of published data and limited interviews of regular *Khat* users revealed that *Khat* chewing lowers libido in humans and may lead to sexual impotence following long-term use. In pregnant women, consumption of *Khat* affects growth of fetus by inhibiting utero-placental blood flow and as a consequence, impairs fetal growth (Mwenda *et al*, 2003: 318).

Dr Solomon Teferra[5], who is in a position to know, testifies in unequivocal terms regarding the damage caused by *Khat* consumption to human health in general and

---

[5] Associate Professor, Department of Psychiatry, Addis Ababa University; Consultant Psychiatrist and Specialist in Addiction Psychiatry, Zewditu Memorial Hospital.

mental health in particular in his very recent article on the subject. On the basis of the 2006 report by WHO Expert Committee on Drugs, he lists the organ or systems affected by *Khat*, which includes all of the vital ones, i.e.: the *cardiovascular* (tachycardia, palpitations, hypertension, arrhythmias, vasoconstriction, myocard infarction, cerebral hemorrhage, pulmonary edema), *central nervous* (dizziness, impaired cognitive functioning, fine tremor, insomnia, headaches), *gastro-intestinal* (dry mouth, polydipsia, dental caries, periodontal disease, chronic gastritis, constipation, hemorrhoids, paralytic ileus, weight loss, duodenal ulcer, upper gastro-intestinal malignancy), *genito-urinary* (urinary retention, spermatorrhoea, spermatozoa malformations, impotence, libido change), *hepatobiliary* (fibrosis, cirrhosis), and *respiratory systems* (tachypnoea, bronchitis); and adds to these, *metabolic and endocrine effects* (hyperthermia, perspiration, hyperglycaemia), and *obstetric effects* (low birth weight, stillbirths, impaired lactation) (Solomon Tefera, 2016:7).

The above list is too comprehensive to ask for more by way of verifying the perception of this study's informants concerning the impacts of *Khat* on the health of members of their communities. Yet, what Solomon Tefera states concerning the effects of *Khat* on the mind specifically, deserve special mention here:

> The deleterious effect of *Khat* on the mind has been a subject of interest for many researchers. Several reports confirmed *Khat's* ability to cause psychological dependence. In chronic *Khat* chewers, withdrawal symptoms that involve frightening dreams locally termed as *Dukak,* which last for one to two nights were reported to occur. The *Dukak* reported by individuals suffering from *Khat* withdrawal tend to be very frightening and dramatic. Some individuals report being crashed and put in a bottle or held upside down and tortured by a ghost who would usually interrogate them why they didn't chew *Khat*. They also feel very depressed and irritable (may start a fight easily). They become lethargic (low energy), feeling hot in lower extremities and the desire (craving) to chew *Khat*.

> More severe psychological reactions such as psychoses were reported as well. In a review published in 2007, Warfa reported more than twenty cases of *Khat*-induced psychosis. It was difficult to establish a causal relationship, but the onset of psychotic symptoms was temporally related with *Khat* chewing. The most common manifestation of amphetamine intoxication is psychosis. Although cathionone is a weak amphetamine

and the amount taken from chewing the *Khat* leaves is usually small, some individuals who consume large amount of *Khat* for days being sleep deprived exhibited acute psychotic symptoms. There was a case report of a 55 year-old Ethiopian who chewed *Khat* for three consecutive days, sleep deprived, and developed acute psychotic episode. At the peak of this *Khat* induced psychosis he murdered his wife and daughter. He was diagnosed with "*Khat* narcomania" (Solomon Tefera, 2016: 9).

In sum, in the minds and narratives of individuals who suffer from mental disabilities, their families, their psychiatrists, and the society at large, addiction to or dependence on *Khat* is intricately linked to the human ill health in general and mental disabilities in particular.

The mechanisms and the trajectories through which *Khat* adversely impacts human health, are, however, not limited to the chemical effects of that the masticated substance on the organs and systems of its chewers alone. One other route is through its impact on health workers, which then reduces the provision of health services. In Assosa, health workers too, chew *Khat* negatively affecting their ethical standard and performance level. To this effect, in the course of the Education & Health Officers' FGD, Ato Tekalign Daka, the Health Bureau's TB Focal Person, stated that health workers in Assosa also chew *Khat* and that has impacted both their ethics and performance. Thus the health service in Assosa is obviously impacted by *Khat* due to its incapacitating effect on health workers.

It is noteworthy, however, that in spite of the burden under which the health service in the city finds itself, Assosa Hospital was so well aware and concerned of the seriousness of the problem of *Khat* addiction in the city, that it came to avail some of its already limited resources for the purpose of housing the joint *Khat* rehabilitation center within its premises —concerning which more is said in Section 3.

2.2.5   Education and educational institutions

Whereas *Khat* impacts nearly all levels of the educational setup, it has a very special and close relationship with the tertiary level ones. Hence, this section presents the findings of the study regarding the impacts of *Khat* on education and educational institutions in Assosa, first, in general, and then, as it pertains to the tertiary level in particular.

2.2.5.1 Education and educational institutions in general

The study has learnt that the consumption of *Khat* has become widespread among the educational community of Assosa, by spreading from teachers to students as well as along peer group network. It has had serious counter disciplinary consequences that have detrimental consequences for the teaching-learning process, as indicated by the high dropout rate, school absenteeism and tardiness. Delinquent acts such as theft and destruction of school property by *Khat* dependent students have become quite common. All of these have resulted in the decline of the quality of education in general.

A participant in the CS-FGD, Ato Belay, stated that teachers not only send their own students to buy *Khat* for them, but even sit and chew *Khat* together with their students. He added school absenteeism, dropping out of school, and quarrels with parents are becoming more common among young people following the spread of the habit amidst them.

Education & Health FGD: Ato Melkamu Tadesse (Deputy Head of the Education Bureau) said that *Khat* has caused many problems in the education sector. There is higher dropout rate, late coming, and delinquency as many children are involved in the *Khat* business, and some even chew it. He states that children/youth who chew *Khat* are caught stealing and destroying school property. He concluded by saying that such students don't maintain good hygiene, they isolate themselves, avoid family members, and are in general asocial.

Ato Melkamu also believes that *Khat* spreads to students from their teachers who often send them to buy *Khat*. In addition to teachers, he argued, other *Khat* chewing people such as contractors and drivers serve as negative role models for the youth.

2.2.5.2 Tertiary-level education and educational institutions

Assosa University, which is the major tertiary-level educational institution in city, has proved to be a prominent vehicle in spreading the habit of chewing *Khat*. Migratory cycles that bring to Assosa ever newer batches of students from the various parts of the country where the practice of *Khat* consumption is well entrenched, facilitates the spread of the habit in waves that start but do not stop at the gate of the University's campus. Furthermore, the extreme physical proximity engendered by the campus pattern of residence, together with the enormous pressure under which most students labor, facilitates the swift contagion of the habit.

Ato Getahun Abdissa Lencha, Vice-president for Administration of Assosa University, confirmed that students chew *Khat* in the university compound, even though the university doesn't allow it. They also chew *Khat* freely in cafés out of campus. The basic reason given by many students being that it helps them to study harder.

Local events have also contributed to the spread of *Khat* use among the University community, according to the Vice-president for Administration. Certain households that were displaced to make room for the construction of the city's stadium were given plots of land adjacent to the university campus on which to build residential houses. But some of them immediately converted the hastily put up cabins and shacks into *Khat bets* thereby providing the *Khat* using university community that is located far away from the city with the closest and easiest possible access to the substance.

Around one-third (30–40%) of the 1,200 staff of the University and many of its guards regularly chew *Khat* —by the estimate of its Dean of Students. Some of the academic and administrative staffs are heavily addicted to *Khat* to the extent of being unable to undertake their tasks normally. According to the Acting Vice-president for Academic Affairs, Ato Tekel Alemnew, in one telling instance, an addict instructor abruptly left a seminar in the middle of the presentation of an academic paper, as he could not control his craving for *Khat*.[6]

The adverse impact of *Khat* consumption on Assosa University has been as pronounced as the latter's role in spreading the habit. Delinquent behavior engendered by *Khat* that borders on criminality has hindered the University's ability to accomplish its educational mission of teaching, learning and research.

According to the three high ranking officials of the University who participated in an FGD on the topic of *Khat*, students originating from areas where *Khat* is chewed, introduce it to other fellow students and help create a market for it inside and around the University campus. The consumption of *Khat* among students of the University is

---

[6] In their study on 'Khat chewing and its socio-demographic correlates among the Staff of Jimma University', Yeshigeta Gelaw and Abraham Haile-Amlak reached the following conclusion that is in line what was learnt from our informants both in Assosa and Harar regarding the widespread consumption of *Khat* by staff of tertiary educational institutions, the failures in their duty, and the role they play in spreading the habit of *Khat* chewing: "A fairly large proportion of Jimma University staff, which are assumed to be models for the rest of the population, chew *Kha*t and this has a strong negative impact on service delivery and the teaching-learning process as they miss their regular work because of the practice" (Yeshigeta Gelaw and Abraham Hile-Amlak, 2004: 179).

very high, and carried on within the University campus in spite of existing regulation against it.

According to Assosa University Dean of Students, Ato Getachun Assefa,

> Theft of shoes, clothes, mobiles, and even laptops are reported to the Office of the Dean of Students, and when these are investigated, the perpetrators usually turn up to be *Khat* addicts. There have been frequent instances of university guards, who, having caught students trying to smuggle *Khat* into the University, simply let them go free. This is because such guards themselves are chewers. We also get reports of theft of shoes, clothes, mobiles, and even laptops. When we investigate these cases, we find out that the perpetrators are usually *Khat* addicts who get to commit criminal acts in order to cover their *Khat* related expenses.

The same well-placed informant confirmed that the consumption of *Khat* and crimes associated to it have escalated among the University student population. The situation has gone too far, to the extent that in one extreme case, a group of students went to a farm that is located behind the University campus to steal *Khat*, and when the owner of the farm spotted and run after them, one of the students that he caught, got into a fight with him and was killed.

Regarding measures, he reported that the university is part of the taskforce set-up to fight *Khat* at the city level. The ethics and anticorruption club in the university also teaches students not to chew *Khat*. But the University can't effectively implement the regulation against brining *Khat* into its campus, as it is not yet fenced.

Ato Melkamu Tadesse, Deputy Head of the Education Bureau, stressed the contribution of universities in popularizing the consumption of *Khat*, and added the dramatic statement that the country has "lost a generation of educated people as a result of the Italian invasion, a second one due to the Red Terror, and now we are losing a third generation to *Khat*"!

2.2.6 Crime and correction

Khat has acted as the gateway to many social ills that have spread to the same extent as that of its consumption. Theft, domestic disturbance, and fights, are now all common among *Khat* addicts and at the *Khat* market. Some police officers and guards who are *Khat* dependent themselves, protect *Shisha* bar owners and students who bring *Khat* into campuses; and as a result of their actions or commissions, some have left their jobs or were dismissed.

CS-FGD participant Ato Belay stated that *Khat* is a gateway to many social ills. For instance, in Mao-Komo, theft that was once considered *Haram* and something in which people rarely engaged has lately become widespread on account of its use and addiction.

In the course of the Anti-Corruption Commission & Police Commission-FGD, Deputy Inspector Hagos Yeshak remarked that,

> The Police receive many complaints that are *Khat* related. Theft, domestic disturbance, and fights, are all common among *Khat* addicts particularly at the *Khat* market. We usually go to the *Khat* market to look for suspected thieves, as it is their usual hangout.

The Deputy Inspector further disclosed that, "there are cases of persons [policemen] who have resigned from the Force on account of their addiction to *Khat*".

2.2.7 Civil service delivery

Widespread addiction to or dependence on *Khat* among civil servants has gravely impaired the delivery of civil service in Assosa. Firstly, such civil servants are not attentive to their work, and the public for whom their services are absolutely essential suffers from their failure in duty. Secondly, as the cost of *Khat* can't be borne with the salary of most government workers, civil servants who are addicts are forced to engage in corrupt practices in order to finance their *Khat* habit.

A participant in the CS-FGD, Ato Belay, stated that *Khat* chewing is so widespread among civil servants and officials that when those seeking their services can't find these persons in their offices, they will have to find out where they frequently chew *Khat* in order to go there and get their affairs sorted out.

Ato Belay went on to relate the case of his ex-colleague who being a *Khat* addict was always taking loans in order to buy *Khat*. As he had so many creditors he could only pay some of them whenever he received his monthly salary, and thus had to run away and hide from his other creditors at the beginning of every month. He eventually suffered from mental illness and quit his job.

CS-FGD participants agreed that many civil servants are addicts, unable to work with focus after 10:00 AM, as a result of *Harara*. They argued that since cost of *Khat* cannot be covered with government salary, civil servants who are addicts are likely to engage in shady acts.

Another participant of the CS-FGD, Ato Ashenafi, reported that he knows two government employees who have been dismissed from their jobs due to repeated absenteeism as a result of *Khat* addiction.

Ato Solomon Abetew, Family Planning Officer and Research & Ethics Committee member of the Health Bureau, disclosed the following:

> There are many civil servants in Assosa, who spend a lot of time, even during working hours, chewing *Khat* and drinking alcohol afterwards to counteract the effects the *Khat*. The problem was so severe; the Regional government even took measures to close *Khat bet* once before. But, it is difficult to control these and *Shisha bet* in Assosa because even police officers that are expected to control it are in league with their owners. Thus, the latter get information about any impending search campaign through the officers and simply melt away before the planned action could take place.

Diakon Tehetena Abebe, Church Development Coordinator, observed:

> There is a serious problem with *Khat*, in that persons in high religious and government post are themselves *Khat* dependent and are setting the wrong example as role models. Furthermore, some police officers cooperate with *Shisha* operators by tipping them ahead of planned raids, so that they will get rid of incriminating evidence by moving their equipments and supplies to a different place.

Ato Tesfaye Nemera, Assosa City Revenue Office, Revenue Collection Process Owner confirms the above, in the following terms:

> It is difficult to control the *Shisha* service here because even police officers that are expected to control it are in league with the owners. Thus, they get information about any impending search campaign and simply melt away before the planned action is taken.

2.2.8   Concerning *Khat's* positive impacts – or the lack of them – in Assosa

In order not to bias the findings of the study, informants were first let to come up spontaneously with any positive socioeconomic impacts that *Khat* may have on the people of Assosa. Then, whenever they failed to do so unsolicited, they were prodded to think in those directions by being reminded of the possibilities. Surprisingly enough, repeated efforts made in this line of enquiry did not produce tangible results, as informants were adamant in stressing that they do not and cannot conceive of any positive effect of *Khat* on their city and its people.

However, it would be fare to report in this final paragraph of a section that has dealt with the various socioeconomic impacts of *Khat* on Assosa, that the study informants also failed to mention even some of the hazardous effects of *Khat* that one often comes across in the literature. Thus, they did not mention either the obvious contribution of *Khat* plants to the rural environment in reducing soil erosion nor its opposite impact on the urban environment by way of contribution to excessive solid waste production; its positive social facilitation service that is acclaimed as its big plus by some writers (Pantelis *et al* 1989: 659, Kennedy, 1987) nor its alleged hunger suppression effect (Lemieux *et al*, 2014). The latter phenomenon, particularly in its excessive form, is actually treated as a negative outcome by some writers as it borders with anorexia (Kennedy, 1987: 130).

Lastly, it is worth noting some relevant socioeconomic impacts that were not brought up by the study informants in Assosa. Informants of the study, here, did not raise such well-known health hazards of *Khat* as oral cavity problems (Kennedy, 1987: 222-3), which they possibly thought of as too obvious to deserve mentioning, or its effects on pregnant and lactating women, regarding which they were probably not clear enough.

2.3   Measures Underway in Assosa to Curb the Escalating *Khat* Consumption & Addiction, and to Treat & Rehabilitate Addicts

It is already made clear in the preface and the Subsection dealing with the study's objective, that the second major purpose of this study was to identify and assess the measures undertaken by governmental and non-governmental agents – including the two partner NGOs – to counteract the spread of *Khat* consumption and addiction and/or to rehabilitate addicts. This section and the one that follows it present the findings of the study in this regard.

2.3.1   Measures undertaken by governmental organizations

Informants drawn from the relevant Benishangul-Gumuz Regional Government Bureaus and Assosa City Administration Offices were in agreement that while the problem of *Khat* abuse, addiction and the socioeconomic problems associated with them are fast getting out of control, very little is being done by government organizations in order to reverse the trend. The only involvement of government organizations in this regard is so far limited to the membership of two of them (BoLSA and BoWCYA) in the Taskforce organized through the initiative of BGDAN for the purpose curbing the spread of *Khat* consumption & addiction and rehabilitating addicts. Besides, as this Taskforce was not yet active at the time of the fieldwork informing the study, the activities in which these government agencies had so far participated in, were limited to the facilitation of the work of the CSOs and participation in some of the awareness creation events.

Wz. Freheiwot Abebe Gobena, Deputy Head of the BoWCYA had this to say:

> We have taken awareness raising measures to combat the spread of *Khat*. We also work with BGDAN as a member of the city level steering committee. As part of the service we render to the youth, we have established recreation centers in 10 *Wäräda*. But that is not enough. We have to raise their awareness about drugs and addiction so that they would spend time in the recreation centers instead of in places where drugs are consumed. We also want to work in high schools to raise awareness of *Khat* by working with clubs. More research is necessary to understand the scale, causes, and consequences of *Khat* chewing in the Region. The bureau already had preliminary discussion with Assosa University to have research done on *Khat*, even by students. The government needs to realize that an entire generation is being lost to *Khat* in favor of foreign exchange. Who is going to inherit the land, foreign exchange or the people (ለወደፊቱ፡ ሀገር የሚረከበው የውጭ ብር ነው ወይስ ሰው)? A national policy on *Khat* is needed, because even if *Khat* is stopped here, it can spread into other regions. Concerted action is vital.

Ato Mesfin Bekele Tulu, Developmental Social Welfare Case Team Leader, and Ato Abebe Senbeta, Social Rehabilitation and Resource Mobilization Officer of BoLSA, passed on the following information:

> Our Bureau has limited capacity as it works with only 8 staff. Most of the resource the Bureau gets is for rehabilitation and transformation of all vulnerable groups. BoLSA is not working specifically on *Khat* addicts,

but on all of those who are vulnerable to various addictions in 10 *Wärädä* of the Region (Some 300 persons) spending 3,500 Birr per person as a revolving fund for IGA. As a result it focuses its work on other urgent vulnerabilities, such as that of people living with HIV and AIDS. Thus, it does not work on its own on *Khat* addiction, but together with other partners in the taskforce on Community Care Coalition (CCC) of which it is a member and which it organized. The Bureau undertakes capacity building for rehabilitation and facilitates the work of other partners.

Also, recently the BoLSA has become a member of the *Khat* Taskforce established following the advocacy work of BGDAN, but it doesn't involve directly in project implementation or rehabilitation of *Khat* addicts. The Bureau has little data on the state of addiction and related problems in the Region. Rehabilitation of addicts is a costly undertaking that cannot be financed by the government. Thus, the Bureau has so far only provided irregular and minor support to *Khat* addicts such as writing them support letters when they try to solicit aid from potential benefactors. Even when *Khat* addicts are involved in some IGA projects of the Bureau, this is not done for addicts as a specific group but along with being members of other vulnerable groups.

2.3.2 Measures undertaken by civil society organizations

2.3.2.1 *The setup*

CSSP Western (Ethiopia) Regional Business Unit operates from its Head Office in Assosa and covers Benishangul-Gumuz NRS, Gambella NRS, West Oromia and West Amhara (but not yet active in the latter one). The Unit works with a coalition of CSOs of which one is its lead partner and others are implementers (being direct and indirect grantees of the program). Benishangul-Gumuz Development Association Network (BGDAN) is the lead organization that has other organizations (direct implementers) working on *Khat* under it. These are:

- Assosa Environment Protection Association (AEPA)
- Tesfa Belechta Association (TBA)
- Education for Development Association (EDA)
- Mao-Komo Development Association, and
- Mujuju Waloca (Women Development) Association

2.3.2.2   Measures Undertaken

The coalition of CSOs that is sponsored by CSSP and led by BGDAN undertook activities aimed at awareness creation, mobilization and the provision of treatment and rehabilitation in and attempt to reverse the spread of *Khat* abuse and help some of its victims out of their dire situation. The same way as other CSO/NGO initiatives, this too is meant to identify effective best practices that can be picked, improved upon, and propagated by other change agents chief of which is government. It is with this perspective of *trailblazer* role that the limited but lofty measures undertaken by the coalition must be assessed. To date, the coalition has carried out the following major activities:

- Awareness raising training has been given on *Khat* and its correlates to 1,010 people.

- Awareness raising anti-*Khat* messages communicated to the public through publication such as *Let us Create a Generation that is Khat Clean* and *Khat Clean Citizen for Development* (Benishangul-Gumuz Development Organizations Coalition. Lisane-Limat. 2014 No. 4 & 2015 No. 5. Assosa)

- Life skill training was provided for 430 youth

- Anti-drug clubs have been strengthened /established

- Strengthening youth centers – Mao-Komo

- 150 farmers in 5 *Wäräda* s are involved in an effort to reduce the production of *Khat* by giving them high value replacement crops, such as apple, to plant[7]

- Youth have been organized into small enterprises to engage in income generation activities

- A regional television program is being aired on Tuesdays and Saturdays

- Most significantly, rehabilitation of *Khat* addicts in collaboration with Assosa Hospital. At the time of the study the first batch had graduated and a second batch was under treatment, and

---

[7] This measure appears to have led towards reducing the rate at which *Khat* production was expanding, if not towards effectively reversing the upward trend. By way of example, a farmer in Bambassi is reported as having replaced 5 hectares of *Khat* plantation with improved-seed maize. We were also told that another farmer in the same area gave up the idea of planting *Khat* as a result of the training he was given, after he had dug 4,200 holes to plant *Khat*.

- Ex-addicts and rehabilitated addicts have been supported to be organized and operate in micro & small enterprises (MSEs).

2.3.2.3 *Treating and Rehabilitating Addicts*

The five-months rehabilitation program run as a joint initiative of BGDAN and Assosa Hospital, and housed inside the premises of the latter, is a genuine trailblazer for other regions of the country in more ways than one. In spite of its short duration and limited funding, it has successfully rehabilitated some 45 *Khat* addicts giving them a fresh lease on life. The program operated as five distinct one-month cycles each of which accepted and treated a batch of 9 addicts on voluntary basis. The exploratory study trip and the major fieldwork trip of this study fortunately coincided with the graduation ceremony of the first cycle batch and the third week of the second cycle respectively; and thus allowed the study to gain a closer association with the rehabilitees and deep insight about them and the program.

Ato Derbachew Melkamu, Head Psychiatrist of the Mental Health Department of Assosa General Hospital and in Charge of the Program, assessed the program as follows:

> Participants in the rehabilitation program have showed positive changes. Only one individual dropped out in the first round, and that due to mistake committed during his recruitment giving him the impression that he would be paid a daily allowance. No one dropped out from the second round.

The program could be improved by providing proper space for the rehabilitation participants and availing separate space for male and female patients. A mental health ward separate from the current rehabilitation ward is needed. Also, longer treatment time is needed.

Furthermore, risks of relapsing due to pressure from drug using peers, idleness, and the like have to be overcome. Attention must be given to the family, since the family has a central role in preventing rehab graduates from relapsing. As for the fate of the program, only ownership of the program by the government would guarantee its sustainability.

2.3.3 Challenges faced and threats anticipated in realising measures

The list below summarizes the challenges in and threats to reversing the spread of *Khat* addiction and creating conducive atmosphere for the rehabilitation of addicts and heavy users. The challenges, in no order of primacy, are:

The main challenges faced by the program in general were the following:

- Lack of policy and regulation governing the production, marketing, and consumption of *Khat* for the region as well as for the country was raised by virtually all informants as being the major stumbling block for the program

- The fact that *Khat chewing is common among* high-level government officials, police officers and professionals who would be in charge of any region or citywide intervention, and

- Short duration and unsustainable funding of the program was felt as the main threat for the program nearly by all – government officials and community leaders included.

As for the rehabilitation sub-program the challenges/shortcomings are:

- Peer pressure on those that attempt to kick off the habit/addiction
- Lack of proper space for the rehab participants and availing separate space for male and female patients
- Absence of a mental health ward separate from rehabilitation ward
- The very short treatment time allotted for rehab
- Absence of full commitment and ownership by government that could improve it and guarantee its sustainability, and
- Short duration and unsustainable funding was likewise considered the major threat for this pioneer sub-program, the end of which was already looming at the time of the fieldwork and was being lamented by all concerned parties.

Moreover, not surprisingly, the quick and high income that is derived from growing *Khat* that makes farmers reluctant to give up this practice easily renders the crop replacement sub-program quite challenging.

2.4 To Hell and Back with the "Flower of Paradise": Voices from Assosa Rehabilitation Centre

In the belief that there is nothing as insightful as subjects' own descriptions of the journeys they traversed first in getting into the *Khat* trap and then escaping from it through gaining awareness and receiving rehabilitation, case stories that have been garnered during the fieldwork are hereunder presented. Whereas some of the stories are offered, as told by the subjects themselves, in their own words, few are presented in paraphrased form, with the subjects of the stories being referred to in the third person. Regardless of this variation in the modality of the presentation, the bases of the narratives are, in both cases, the taped interviews and observation notes pertaining to each of the case stories.

2.4.1 The case of Ato M. G, a 31 year-old graduate of Adama University in Business Management, and an addict under treatment in the Rehabilitation Centre, and brother of Wz. G. G.

He first started with drinking alcohol, and stopped drinking because his health was deteriorating. He then moved to chewing *Khat*, as a replacement to his alcohol drinking. He also smokes, and said that he spends, on the average, around 100 Birr per day on *Khat* and its attendant substances and stuff. This was too much for his means, and he was able to support his habits only because of friends who subsidized him.

He maintained only limited relation with his family, as he spent most of his time in *Khat* dens and with *Khat* friends. He said, "I would leave home at dawn, to get back only late at night. I would go home to sleep or only if I needed to change my cloth."

He is worried that he might slip back to chewing *Khat* once he comes out of the rehabilitations unless he stops hanging out with his current friends.

Wz. G. G, Sister of the above-described Ato M. G, speaks:

My brother didn't chew *Khat*, drink alcohol, or smoke cigarettes until he passed the Grade-12 examination and went to Adama University.

He hasn't shown any improvement financially or otherwise since his graduation. He doesn't look after himself. He also avoids us (family and relatives) because we advise him to stop chewing *Khat*. When he started to totally avoid us, we stopped giving any advice.

When the rehabilitation program opened, I asked him to participate, but he resisted. He kept on saying that he doesn't have a problem with addiction. Even after he agreed to come here, he was very reluctant to participate.

2.4.2 The case of Ato S.T, an addict under treatment in the Rehabilitation Centre, and husband of Wz. F.N

First, I started smoking cigarette at the age of 7 while living in Sudan with the OLF that had snatched me from home. I came back to Ethiopia and to my parents in 1992, and then I started chewing *Khat* in 1996 in Beghi, where it is produced abundantly. People there would start chewing *Khat* early in the morning even before having breakfast. I used to work as a semi-skilled worker earning an average of 200 Birr/day, but I would spend most of it on *Khat* inviting my friends to it. I used to quarrel with my wife over my chewing habit because I used to spend most of my time in recreational places chewing *Khat* and playing pool and bingo.

Last December, Tesfa Belechta Association organized us as 'one-in-five' [following the pattern of the Development Army] and gave us advice to seek help and strive to quit *Khat*. But, some outsiders told us the program was going to get us to use some medicine that would drive us crazy and so on. But, since I joined the treatment 23 days ago, I have completely quit *Khat* and cigarettes and I am certain to remain free of addiction. Now, I have even started to advise friends to stop.

Khat used to create temporary euphoria and made me dream of success, But, just like with alcohol drunkenness all is forgotten the next morning.

As for my experience with sex and chewing *Khat*, it delays ejaculation but does not affect performance. Then some of my friends tell me that they don't get steered toward having sex after chewing *Khat*.

Wz. F.N, wife of the above Ato S.T. for the last 8 years, speaks:

My husband wanted to marry me and therefore converted to Islam. We both had a child each before we married and got two more afterward. We used to have a good relationship.

He started chewing *Khat* after we got married. He also smoked a lot, which I did not know about at the time. I used to work as a cleaner at Bamboo Paradise Hotel, and he worked as a causal semi-skilled worker. He chewed *Khat* and smoked cigarette the whole day and night, and spent up to 100 Birr per day on *Khat* and cigarettes, but did not drink alcohol. Even though he works hard and earns money, the family's economic situation couldn't improve. He was advised to quit chewing *Khat* but wouldn't. I had difficulty raising four kids because he spent all his earnings on *Khat* and cigarette. He was organized in 'one-in-five' in a fashion similar to that of the government's Development Army, and he was sponsored to the rehabilitation program through it, and I pressured him to join.

Now he has spent 23 days in the program as an in-patient. I see that he has improved a lot, which is visible to our eyes. He has changed so much physically that even one of the daughters has noticed it. But he is still irritated.

My family and I love him, and he loves his children. But, he cannot control himself because of his addiction. His friends are all *Khat* abusers and we are planning to keep him away from them. Unless he stays away from them, there is a risk that he will relapse into addiction. My family and I plan to keep him away from them. I want him to change, and I believe Allah has brought this program for my sake.

There is nothing to hide about the sexual incapacity that *Khat* brings on men. It is true. We have to tell the truth: *Khat* makes men impotent.

2.4.3 The case of G.T, a 28 year-old addict under treatment in the Rehabilitation Centre

I graduated with a degree in civil engineering in 2009 from Arba Minch University; worked in Tendaho Sugar Estate's Housing Project in 2010 and at Metekel Zone City Administration during 2011-2013.

Friends who came from Shashemene and Ziway introduced me to the habit of chewing *Khat* at Arba Minch University. Thereafter I chewed *Khat* during the 4 years of my stay at the University. It was not a problem to chew *Khat* in the campus because the guards were lenient.

I continued to chew *Khat* in Tendaho, and chewed even more in Metekel during office hours and every day. I used to take per-diem for fake fieldtrips on which I did not go, and then I would stay away from the office and chew *Khat* hiding somewhere in the city. I spent all the money I made, which was up to 400 Birr per day. I didn't help my family and didn't visit them because I was at odds with them over my addiction.

Soon enough, I left my job in Metekel and came to Assosa. Afterwards, I was employed by the government, but left it when I was accused of corruption. I then returned to live in Assosa. But as I was so much addicted to *Khat*, I did not want to go back to work. I hated work.

I kept on chewing *Khat* for four years in *Khat* houses spending all the money I got. But, as for drinking alcoholic beverages, I had started long before that, at home in Metekel. I continued to drink *Arake* for *Č'äbsi*. Even later, I could not work or do drawing without *Khat*. I had problem with my brothers because of my addition, and visited my family only once after graduation, for Meskel Celebration.

I was employed for a while by MIDROC for 6,000 Birr per month and I used to earn a lot more on the side by working as a consultant on projects. I once made 260,000 Birr by working for a Sudanese investor. Soon enough, I had to leave Assosa as they started arresting people on corruption charges. I went first to Bahr Dar and then to Dessie for no particular reason other than that I happened to find seats on buses going there and in the meantime blew all the money and ended up selling even my two suitcase-full clothing. Finally, I returned to Assosa, got arrested but was discharged, as they could not find any proof of corrupt practices on me.

I came out of prison and started living in the streets. People in Assosa City came to know me as I got around struggling to walk straight, insulted people left and right, etc. Then Ato Derebachew, the chief psychiatrist here, met me in the city and brought me here on the pretext of visiting my friend who was already here. I then joined the treatment program voluntarily, as I was fed up with *Khat* and alcohol.

2.4.4 The case of Ato B.T, a 42 year-old addict currently under treatment in the Rehabilitation Centre

Ato B.T. was a health officer in the Ethiopian Defense Forces. He was born and raised in Wolisso, where *Khat* is commonly grown and chewed. He started chewing *Khat* when he was in grade seven to help him study better. Drinking and smoking followed the *Khat*. He said that *Khat* opens the door for other addictions such as drinking and smoking.

He always used to run out of money as a result of his spending it on the purchase of *Khat* and its attendant substances. Moreover, he used to experience extreme fatigue when he was chewing *Khat*, and had low self-esteem at the work place because he knew that he was underperforming and misbehaving.

Plate 1: *Khat* market in Assossa

Plate 2: Children in *Khat* market in Assosa

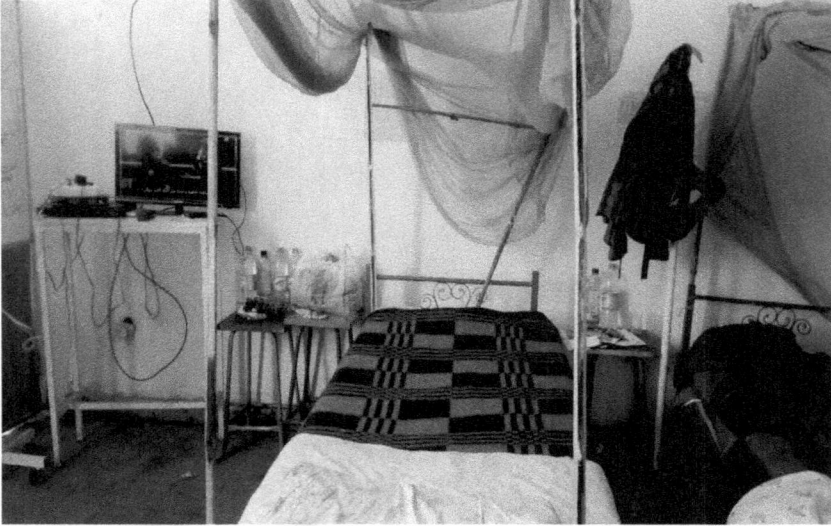

Plate 3: *Khat* rehabilitation ward at Assosa Hospital

Plate 4: Some of the *khat* rehabilees at Asssosa Hospital rehabilitation ward (August, 2015)

His addiction worsened when he came to Assosa in 2003, leaving his wife behind to live with her parents in Addis Ababa. He said that, once in Assosa, he got out of control (መረን ተለቀቅኩ) as there was nobody to watch over him.

He was eventually dismissed from his work with the Armed Forces (about seven months before the date of this interview) and had to live on his savings, and when these were used up, on peoples' charity.

2.4.5 The case of three rehabilitated addicts (1st Round Graduates of the Rehabilitation Centre at Assosa Hospital) residing in Kurmuk Town during the fieldwork

Ato Annous: has remained *Khat* free for a month after graduating from the Assosa Hospital rehabilitation center. In fact, he is trying to teach others and help them quit *Khat*. He avoids places where *Khat* is chewed. He recognizes the economic benefits of stopping to chew *Khat*:

> It is now nearly a month since I took my salary, and I still have 50 Birr in my pocket. I used to quarrel with my wife several times a month, now she is very happy, as we don't fight any more. Our family life has improved a lot.

Ato Abraham reported several positive changes that occurred after he has stopped chewing *Khat*, which he describes in detail as follows:

> I used to eat once a day and then chew *Khat* the whole day. My appetite has improved now. I eat regularly; I even have a snack once in a while. I got divorced with my first wife, with whom I had a baby, as a result of *Khat*. We used to fight a lot because I felt that it was my right to chew *Khat*, and I didn't pay her the necessary attention. I married for a second time, but I used to fight with her also. My life has improved after I stopped chewing *Khat*. I eat well, go home early, and even smell better. I don't run out of money now. Yet, I am facing challenges, as my friends still don't believe that I have truly stopped chewing *Khat*. Some people try to provoke me by inviting me to chew with them, and others mock me for stopping chewing *Khat*. Of course some of these people don't like the fact that I don't chew *Khat* anymore because I don't buy *Khat* for them now.

Ato Abbas used to smoke tobacco, chew *Khat*, and drink alcohol. He considers himself to be the most addicted person there has ever been. He says, "there was no better addict than me" (በሱስ የሚበልጠኝ ሰው አልነበረም). He said he once made 25,000 Birr from traditional gold mining but spent it all on *Khat*, cigarettes, and drinks within two short weeks. But now, he says, his financial situation has greatly improved. He has gone back to making his living by engaging in traditional gold mining; and now puts the money he makes to the good use of his family.

2.4.6 The case of a rehabilitated family: Ato A, a 50 year-old man who used to grow *Khat* for the last 30 years and consume it for the last 18, and his primary wife

As a result of the awareness he acquired through the intervention of Mao-Komo Development Association, he significantly reduced his consumption of *Khat*, and abandoned *Khat* production. He only chews *Khat* when guest bring it to his house; and has replaced his *Khat* plantation with apple trees and other fast growing and high value plants.

He said he sleeps better and has good appetite after reducing *Khat* chewing. He also states that he has better marital relationship with his two wives now.

His first wife who begun chewing *Khat* little by little, when she sat with him and received small bits of *Khat* leaves from his hands, had become dependent on *Khat* and developed poor appetite and insomnia. She said that she has now completely stopped chewing *Khat* and is in better physical and mental conditions. She also confirmed that her marital relationship and family life has also improved following her husband's reduction of his *Khat* consumption and her own shaking off of the habit completely.

2.4.7 The case of Ato A.K., a recovered ex-addict and a person living with HIV

In 1990, he started chewing *Khat* little by little, as he run purchase errands for his older brothers who regularly chewed *Khat*. He dropped out of school when he reached Eighth Grade, and joined the Defense Forces. But, as he continued to chew *Khat* even then, he left the Armed Forces and soon after found out that he is HIV positive. He continued to chew *Khat* even long after he was on medication for his condition. He has now stopped chewing *Khat*, thanks to his membership in *Tesfa Bilichta* Association, and is in fact teaching others to do the same.

3 Escalating Consumption & Addiction, Socioeconomic Impacts of *Khat*, and Attempts at addressing them in Harar

Before getting into the introduction, prevalence and socioeconomic impacts of *Khat* in Harar, a brief presentation the current demographic profiles the city and its surrounding Regional State are in order.

The City of Harar is the capital of the Harari People's National Regional State, which is the homeland of the Harari people. The city with its old walled core (Jegol) at its centre has remained a trading hub as well as a center of Islamic religion and education that connected the Eastern Ethiopian Highlands with the Arabian Peninsula and the Middle East for over a Millennium. Harar was object of fascination for foreign travelers including Sir Richard Burton who believed that the city and its environs were the birthplace of *Khat* that was only later introduced into Yemen. He describes with loads of superlatives the image of the city that beckoned him and other adventures as follows:

> The ancient metropolis of a once mighty race, the only permanent settlement in Eastern Africa, the reported seat of Moslem learning, a walled city of stone houses, possessing its independent chief, its peculiar population, its unknown language, and its own coinage, the emporium of the coffee trade, the head-quarters of slavery, the birth-place of the Kat plant, and the great manufactory of cotton-cloths, amply, it appeared, deserved the trouble of exploration (Burton, 1856, Vol. I, Preface to the 1856 edition: xxvi).

With a total population of 183,415 (CSA 2008) and an estimated area of some 311 square kilometers, Harari is by far the smallest of the nine national regional states making up the Ethiopian federal state. The city itself accounts for 99,368 or 54% of the Region's ethnically and religiously diverse population. The ethnic groups in the region include the Oromo (56.41%), Amhara (22.77%), Harari (8.65%), Guragie (4.34%), Somali (3.87%), Tigray (1.53%), and Argobba (1.26%). Most of the inhabitants of the Region are Moslems with 69.0%, followed by Ethiopian Orthodox Christians who make up 27.1%, Protestants (3.4%), Catholics (0.3%), and worshipers of other religions (0.2%) (CSA 2008: 112).

The demographic profile of urban Harar taken separately reveals a significant deviation from that of the regional aggregate. The ethnic distribution of the urban population is altered with Amhara constituting 40.55%, Oromo 28.13%, Harari 11.83%, Guragie 7.94%, Somali 6.82%, Tigrai 2.76% and Argoba 0.12% (CSA 2008: 102-3). Religion wise, Ethiopian Orthodox Christians are this time in the lead with 48.6%, closely followed by Moslems (44.6%), and at a distance by Protestants (6.1%), Catholics (0.1%) and all others put together (0.3%) (CSA 2008: 112).

3.1 Introduction into, Spread and Prevalence of *Khat* Consumption & Addiction in Harar

3.1.1 Introduction into and Spread of *Khat* in Harar

It has been learnt from informants that the practice of chewing *Khat* goes far back to times immemorial and had legendary beginnings. Informants said that some people even believe that Harar is in fact the place of origin of *Khat*. Its use is given religious justification and origin by many, as attested by its lofty appellation as the *"Plant/Flower of Paradise"*. While its use by the local Moslem population goes as far back as the history of the area, its spread and predominance among larger segments of the population in general and the non-Harari, non-Oromo and non-Moslem population in particular is by and large a post-1974 phenomenon. Thus, if the spread of *Khat* in Assosa can be considered a *developmental hazard*, that of Harar City is decidedly one of *tradition*.

Ato Wuhib Mohammad of HIAC explained the hold of the claim to religious origin has had on peoples' minds and the attempt to reverse it that is currently being put up as follows:

> There are two opposed views expounded in Harar, both of them associating *Khat* to religion. While one view claims that *Khat* is the *Plant of Paradise*, the other holds that it is in fact the *Headdress of the Devil*. We try to counteract the former and popularize the latter position in working towards the reduction of *Khat* consumption and addiction.

Six religious leaders and community elders, participating in an FGD, stated that the current understanding of the introduction of *Khat* into Harar that has been arrived at through the community conversation program, is that contrary to the belief that it has a religious origin, it was in fact brought in by someone who wanted to keep the city's people inactive and backward.

3.1.2   Prevalence of *Khat* Consumption and Addiction in Harar

Nearly the totality of the study's informants in Harar agreed that the domination of the economic and social life of the city by *Khat* is so overwhelming, as attested by the:

–   Extensive *Khat* plantation surrounding the city, being grown by 88% of the rural households in 2011 (CSA. 2012b: Table 9.1, b)

–   Omnipresence of *Khat* markets and stalls, and

–   Large numbers of persons are "possessed" or "captured" by *Khat* and are seen chewing it all over public places.

The proportion of persons who consume *Khat* and even that of those "captured" by it is so high, that informants use the phrase "everybody" when they speak of all users, and "too many" in reference to those they deem to be is "possessed" or "captured" by *Khat* or happen to be heavy users and addicts.

Ato Tekalegn Mehari, a 65 years-old resident of Dire Dawa and Harar for over 45 years and a high school teacher by profession who used to consume *Khat* until he quit it totally 40 years ago in 1975 explained the meaning of terms used to indicate persons that are "possessed" or "captured", and described the extreme state of addiction in which they find themselves, as follows:

> A *Khat* addict is referred to as *Hambis* in Oromiffa and *Jezba* in Amharic, meaning one who is "possessed" or "captured" by *Khat*. Such persons cannot open their eyes properly and do not have the necessary bowel movements in order to relieve themselves as they wake up in the morning. They need to consume some *Khat* to stimulate their system before they can be able to carry out those physiologically necessary functions. These *Hambis* or *Jezba* are people who are recognized by their communities as persons possessed or captured by *Khat*, and they on their part also accept this status and identity that is assigned to them by the community.

The FGD of six religious leaders and community elders[8] concluded that they believe more than 90% of the men and 50% of the women in Harar are *Khat* chewers. To this,

---

[8] The FGD participants consisted of: 1. Ato Fetih Abdisherif, Afosha Leader 2. Ato Teshome Ayele, Idir Leader 3. Ato Mekonen Gorfu, *Iddïr* Leader 4. *Kesis* Gebremichael Bayeh, Priest of Debere-Genet Medhane-Aleme Church 5. Sheik Muktar Mubarek, Afosha Leader and Head of the Main Mosque 6. Ato Zubeir Hassan, Afocha Leader).

one of the participants added a telling remark, albeit with intentional exaggeration, saying, "In Harar, you have to search with a flashlight to find someone free of *Khat*."[9]

Ato Abdulaziz Mohammad, Youth and Women Mainstreaming and Projects Coordination Process Owner, BoWYCA, said, "The prevalence of *Khat* usage is about 70% in the population of the city. But, this figure includes both those who are addicted and those that are irregular and only social chewers". This percentage of *Khat* chewers among the whole population he provided (70%), renders plausible the gender disaggregated FGD estimates presented in the foregoing paragraph, which is 90% of the men and 50% of the women residents of the city. These estimates are supported by the findings of the national Demographic and Health Survey of 2011, which found, the percentage of respondents who ever chewed chat to be lowest in Tigray (1 percent of women and 4 percent of men) and highest in Harari (39 percent of women and 82 percent of men) (CSA, 2012a: 54).

3.1.3 Patterns of, and factors behind *Khat* consumption and addiction in Harar

The study's informants identified the following 12 factors as having favored the spread of the *Khat* phenomenon to one extent or another:

1. The narrative that upholds *Khat* as a "Plant of Paradise" thereby providing an implied religious justification for its consumption

2. Social permissiveness due to the longstanding association with, acceptance and romanticizing of the use and abuse of *Khat* by the indigenous community that has also gradually influenced the in-migrants

3. The widely held practice of providing children with *Khat* allowance by their parents

4. The established practice of providing children with an atmosphere conducive to *Khat* at home including a special *Khat* chewing room

5. The relatively widespread practice of tolerating young children to consume small amounts of *Khat* from their tender age onwards

---

[9] Interestingly enough, Tim Carmichael reports what he learnt in Harar, which resonates the above as follows:

> Regarding the issue of dependence, everyone I spoke with said it is a problem. It is said to affect men and women, young and old, Moslems and Christians alike. "Most people," in fact, are generally said to have it. For example, when asked if it is common, one man replied, "Yes, as I think you know, almost everyone who goes on two legs has it" (Carmichael, 2000: 56).

6. Easy access to affordable *Khat* due to its abundant production and circulation within the vicinity of the city

7. The established practice of providing *Khat* on credit, on reciprocal donation, and even in the form of free gift

8. Expansion of education, and the resultant inward and outward movements of teachers and students with *Khat* habit

9. Youngsters' emulation of people considered modern or educated, including that of teachers by students

10. The vibrant commercial activity and quick-money-making atmosphere surrounding *Khat,* that acts as a trap leading to the abyss of increased consumption and addiction

11. Rampant unemployment, and

12. Finally, lack of regulation and control.

Khalid Anwar, Advisor on Social Affairs at the Regional President's Office, argued that "*Khat* spreads only when there are enabling factors such as: the substance being easily and cheaply available." The location of Harar City in the middle of a region well known for its *Khat* production as well as between a great *Khat* marketing hub, Aweday Town, and a major export destination, Hargeissa, have conspired together to make it a place of relatively cheap and easily accessible *Khat*.

A second major enabling factor that has contributed towards the high rate of *Khat* consumption in Harar is the common location of its consumption. In Harar, there are very few commercial *Khat*-chewing dens –may be two or three. *Khat* is consumed at home in private chewing rooms that go by the name of *Bärč'a-bet* but are sometime euphemistically referred to by the young as *Tinat-bet*. This has allowed the habit to spread easily among family members including girls and adult women.

There is quite clear class distinction as to where *Khat* is normally consumed. The well-to-do chew their *Khat* in their homes or in those of their friends and relatives, whereas the less fortunate section of the populace including the "possessed" or "captured", the heavy users and addicts chew *Khat* wherever and whenever they get it –mostly in public places such as roadsides, walkways, pedestrian pavements, parks, or any other such open spaces. Ato Hailu Bekele, President of HIAC, further elaborated the class distinction in places of *Khat* consumption, saying:

Khat bet are not common in Harar. Upper and middle class people chew *Khat* at home, while lower class people chew it wherever they find themselves at the hour of chewing – on the streets, at work, under shades, and the like.

A third enabling factor behind the widespread consumption of and addiction to *Khat* in Harar is the practice by which parents openly facilitate and finance their children's *Khat* habit. Ato Selamyehun Aklilu, Director of SID-E, described this phenomenon saying, "Parents indulge their grownup children by providing them regularly with *Mädäb* [a special *Khat* chewing spot at home] and with *Mäshruf* [pocket money that is specifically meant for the purpose of purchasing *Khat*].

Ato Ordin Bedri, Deputy Head of the BoE and member of the Steering Committee on *Khat* Addiction and Prevention, elaborated the reason behind the widespread practice of chewing *Khat* at home as follows:

> There are no commercial *Khat* dens or chewing places in Harar, because here unlike elsewhere in the country, it is common for parents to facilitate the consumption of *Khat* at home by their children, while in other places young people chew *Khat away* from home hiding from their parents. Another reason for the absence of commercial *Khat* dens is that ordinary people customarily chew *Khat* on streets and in public places as well."

A fourth factor that was raised by informants as a major enabler for the spread of *Khat* consumption and addiction is the manner in which it is consumed. Informants maintain that, nowadays, *Khat* is consumed regularly just like meals. It has become common to chew *Khat*, during mourning occasions, weddings and other festivities and social events, as well as during study sessions, etc. The use of *Khat* has become so pervasive that it is quite common for people to take *Khat* with them even when they go to visit hospital in-patients or as *Yä izin* when they go to the house of a bereaved person to pay their respects.

Ato Abdulwassi of HIAC elaborated on this point, as follows:

> *Khat* is now part of the social fabric of Harrar as it is taken to weddings, mourning places, and when elders go to ask for the hand of a girl in marriage, etc. *Khat* chewing is also part of certain religious events. In Abadir and Sheik Hashim shrines, *Khat* is offered by visitors and chewed

by the priesthood to assist them during prayers that often last for whole nights.[10]

Ato Afendi Bashi, Deputy Head of the Health Bureau, pointed out the fact that the location and manner of *Khat* consumption has ultimately contributed to its rising prevalence by bringing within the *Khat* fold additional categories of the population, in the following terms:

> The prevalence of *Khat* consumption has steadily increased in Harar because more and more of the women and elderly folk have joined the young that used to figure prominent in its consumption. Whereas tobacco and alcohol are generally consumed together with *Khat*, women tend to favor *Shisha* and the young are inclined towards smoking cannabis as attendant substances.

A fifth major enabling factor that was repeatedly raised by informants in the course of the fieldwork of this study was the web of mutually supportive habits and addictions that kept the individual in an inescapable stranglehold. Ato Wuhib Mohammad of HIAC noted this, saying,

> The cycle of substance abuse does not end with addiction to *Khat and* its related substances such as *Shisha*, alcohol and cigarettes. It leads to the smoking of cannabis and cannabis.

The connection between *Khat* chewing and cannabis smoking, and their contagious effect on family members are best illustrated by the following story that was told by Ato Muktar, Director of EYNHB:

> There was this elderly lady living in a house where her children regularly burned loaves of cannabis/cannabis resin in an open urn during their *Khat* chewing sessions. Unaware of what was going on, she continued to inhale the smoke and became addicted to, and mentally affected by it. In this way, she became so irrational that one fine day she went to a bank, approached a teller, and demanded payment presenting him her 2015 National Election-voting card as proof of money transferred from abroad by her thoughtful children.

---

[10] Through the good contacts of Ato Abdulwassi, the research team was invited to Sheik Abadir's Shrine where it was allowed to observe the night's prayer ceremony, visit the tombs of the Sheik and other Harari leaders, and was kindly blessed by the assembly.

Yet another factor that was raised by few informants as being behind the spread of *Khat* consumption and addition was the rampant unemployment of the youth in the city. This issue was thoroughly discussed in the FGD of religious leaders and community elders, because there was a strong argument against it. Regarding the contribution of unemployment to the spread of *Khat* consumption and addiction, one of the FGD participants stated that, *"Khat* chewing is facilitated by unemployment, which is in turn driven by population increase in the city". But another individual challenged this view by arguing the contrary, as follows:

> Since the people who seize the employment opportunities that are available are usually those who come from outside of the city, the unemployed status of the chewers is not caused by lack of employment opportunity, but rather by their addiction and lack of interest for work. If you check out the situation at Haromaya University, you will learn that *Khat* chewing, as well as *Shisha,* tobacco and cannabis smoking are wide spread, which is not due to lack of employment as all are either students, teachers or support staff.

Ato Abdulaziz Mohammad, Youth and Women Mainstreaming and Project Coordination Process Owner, BoWYCA, provided an enlightening comparison between the patterns and ways of *Khat* consumption in the past and the present. He remarked:

> There are significant differences between the chewing of *Khat* by the indigenous Harari and Oromo people of the surrounding area in the old days, on the one hand, and that which is practiced these days. The indigenous people used to chew only limited amounts of *Khat* at a time so that it would help them to concentrate on the performance of such tasks as prayers, etc. But, that is not how it is being consumed nowadays.

3.2   Socioeconomic Impacts of *Khat* Consumption and Addiction in Harar

The study has looked into the socioeconomic impacts of *Khat* consumption and addiction in Harar City at the following levels: family life and household economy, women and children, local economy and local community, health, education, crime and its correction, civil servants and civil service delivery.

Overall, the findings of study are unequivocal in reaching the conclusion that *Khat* consumption has very little positive outcomes but many intertwined and symbiotic adverse impacts all along the above listed aspects of societal institutions and social arena.

Ato Abdulaziz Mohammad, Youth and Women Mainstreaming and Projects Coordination Process Owner, BoWYCA, has tried to put the overall positive and negative socioeconomic impacts of *Khat* in Harar City on balance, which deserves to be quoted at some length before getting into the specificities that are listed above:

> The socioeconomic impact of *Khat* on our city is by and large negative; and its adverse impact is becoming more pronounced these days. People are now chewing *Khat* throughout the day and have little time for work and other activities. They are inactive. Many young people have become addicted to *Khat* and also to other allied substances. *Khat* addiction is leading the young to idleness, and theft, particularly if their parents do not afford to foot their *Khat* bills. ·

> As for the positive impact of *Khat*, in the Eastern Ethiopia it is used to bring together several people thereby facilitating social engagements such as discussion of issues of common interest. It should be noted, however, that although *Khat* facilitates social engagement in this regard, this is followed by its ability of leading to over-concentration and self-absorption after a certain amount has been consumed. It makes the group members fixated on certain thoughts, and even become psychotic. This is clearly shown by the number of crazy people one observes on the streets of Harar. *Khat* also has a social function such as being taken as a token of bridal gift by a party that asks the parents of a would-be bride for her hand.

> All in all, unlike in the past, these days, *Khat* results not in heightened efficiency but in inefficiency and lower productivity.

3.2.1 Family life and household economy

Addicts and heavy users access *Khat* in a vicious circle of purchase on credit and credit settlement, ruining their domestic economy and shaming their family. As they are always under pressure by their many ever-relenting creditors, they hide, fight with their spouses, get emotionally disturbed, and ultimately quit or are dismissed from their jobs. Domestic disturbances due to disagreements between spouses; and disputes between parents and children are common. Furthermore, families of *Khat* addicts are forced to foot the health bills of their addict members when they sooner or later fall sick and require medical attention.

Khat dependent wives abuse their households' budget in favor of attending to their habit, and are forced to be secretive in their family and community life. Peer pressure and the permissive tradition that provides for *Bärč'a* rooms in family homes facilitate the process by which women are led into *Khat* dependence and into becoming victims of unethical practices within the family.

Neglect of wives, on several accounts including failure of husbands to fulfill their manly duty, is a major cause of marital discord that often culminate in divorce and family dissolution. Inter-family ties and solidarity weaken, as addict family heads progressively fail to engage in community-wide activities such as visiting the sick, attending burials.

Ato Sissay Dereje, Study, Drafting and Training Core Process Owner in the Bureau of Justice and Security, maintained that,

> The vicious cycle of *Khat* consumption involves: *Khat* chewing – drinking alcohol – smoking cigarette, *Shisha* and/or cannabis – and back to *Khat*. Being so caught in the routines of *Khat,* chewers think of just the day, and therefore, are incapable of providing for their families, let alone being visionary enough to engage in saving.

3.2.2   Women and children

Women are impacted more by the *Khat*-chewing habits of their husbands, as they are the ones responsible for making ends meet and managing their households' economy at all costs. Moreover, *Khat* addicted husbands tend to ignore their wives' emotional and sexual needs.

Children, who are always at the mercy of parents, are the other major victims in *Khat* addicts' families. They carry the short and long-term physical and psychological brunt of the addiction of one or both of their parents to *Khat*. Some are marked by it for life with the likelihood of following in the footsteps of their *Khat* addict parents down the same road. In Harar parents directly or indirectly encourage their children to develop the habit of chewing *Khat* by providing them with special rooms for chewing *Khat* as well as with pocket money earmarked for its purchase. Children's welfare is usually ignored, and in some cases their victimization begins early when they are still in their addict mothers' wombs and continues through the breastfeeding phase of their young lives. (See Box 3, in this Section, for an illustrative case).

Furthermore, what has been learnt by the study from its informants in very general terms in this regard is well-articulated and supported by the medical science literature on *Khat's* hazardous effects on the health of lactating mothers and their offspring.

The six participants in religious leaders and community elders FGD reached consensus regarding the impact of *Khat on* women and the young. Concerning the former, they maintained that the adversity of *Khat* is more pronounced on women as they are the ones who are responsible for managing their households' economy, whereas their *Khat*-chewing husbands who are supposed to be the family providers are least concerned with anything other than getting their *Khat* provisions. Regarding children, the FGD participants held that the practice by which parents provide their children with regular *Khat* money and special chewing rooms has nowadays made the youth of Harar the main consumers of *Khat*.

Chewing *Khat*, and smoking *Shisha*, as well as cannabis in some cases, at home in *Bärč'a* rooms, having become fashionable of late, many women folk are easily slipping into dependence. Wz. Sarah Mohammad, EYNHB Officer, made the following powerful statement concerning the rising *Khat* abuse by women that culminates in their own domestic abuse:

> Chewing *Khat* and smoking have progressively become fashionable among women of Harar. Since having *Bärč'a* rooms in every house is the tradition in the city, it is common for the women folk to easily slip into the habit of regularly consuming *Khat* and get addicted. Attendant substance abuse, particularly that of cannabis is becoming common among women. Consequently, girls are becoming increasingly oblivious towards their personal hygiene. Moreover, women are become easy pray to rape during their *Khat* highs. Incestuous relationships or rapes also take place during or following these home-based *Khat*-chewing vigils. Given these circumstances, some women are driven to suicide.

Ato Tariku Duressa, Vice-President of Harari NRS Supreme Court, lent his opinion, which is supportive of the above:

> Most criminal cases that appear before the High Court in Harar concern domestic abuses, fights, and rapes that are fuelled by *Khat*. They are crimes related to *Khat* economics and committed among family members or relatives who pick fights on account of ownership of *Khat* land, etc. ... Also rape by family members, including that of daughters by their fathers [intergenerational rape] is committed under *Khat Märqana*. The Court

has dealt with incestuous rape cases in which the accused confess that they have committed the crimes under *Khat Märqana*.

There are also many divorce cases, most of which are related to *Khat* and attendant substance consumption by one of the partners. *Khat* leads to sexual impotence, and it is behind many divorce cases that the Court deals with, although the Revised Family Law does not require a plaintive to disclose the cause behind a request to divorce [and is therefore not possible to put a figure on such *Khat* induced divorces].

Ato Abdulaziz Mohammad, Youth and Women Mainstreaming and Projects Coordination Process Owner, BoWYCA, said male *Khat*-chewers give more attention, care and love to *Khat* rather than their families leading to family disruption. And added that the sexual impotence of men that is brought about by *Khat* chewing, further contributes to the plight of wives.

Box 3: *Khat* and the family life of 27-year-old Wz. B.Y, a casual cleaning and laundrywoman, married and mother of three, and a heavy *Khat* addict

She is 27 years old, married and with 3 children. She got into the habit of chewing *Khat* as her mother used to give her *Khat* as medication for minor ailments when she was very young. She has chewed *Khat* as far back as she can recall.

She admits to chew *Khat* almost for whole days and seven days a week, if she gets it. She said she chews *Khat* because it energizes her (ያበረታታኛል). She continued chewing even during her three pregnancies. She laughingly said that she had *Khat* in her mouth even when she was in labor in the delivery room giving birth to her last baby-girl, in spite of the objection of the female doctor attending her.

By her own admission, she is a heavy addict who says she faces no problem while chewing *Khat*, but rather with the withdrawal symptoms such as the shaking of her hands whenever she skips chewing it. She says that she is totally dependent on *Khat* to do her day-to-day activities properly and. Her hands shake if she doesn't chew *Khat*. Once, she seriously attempted to quit it together with her husband who also chews *Khat*, but as she suffered from *Dukak* and horrifying hallucinations she went back at it almost immediately.

She regrets the fact that she was introduced to *Khat* at a young age and wouldn't want her children to chew *Khat*. She wishes for some way to stop chewing *Khat*.

Her third and last child, whom she had brought along with her, had very thin discolored hair; and both mother and the child were disheveled and unclean.

The peculiar impact of *Khat* chewing on women, via its linkage with waitressing and sex-work is more or less the same as that in Assosa, a subject already discussed under Section 2.2.2, and is therefore not repeated here. However, it worth mentioning what has been learnt in the course of an FGD with a group of three sex-workers that was being supported by SID-E to quit both sex-work and chewing *Khat* and instead start a small restaurant as a group. While two of the group's members appeared to be willing to continue with the project, provided they received continued support, the third member was adamant that she would never be able to stop chewing *Khat* no matter what the future holds for her. She in fact left the discussion declaring her being resigned to her fate.

Likewise, *Khat* has also a special impact on children and youth that are forced to fend for themselves for various reasons, including parental addiction to *Khat,* and forced to engage in the easily available work of *Khat Makär*. These unfortunate individuals work in warehouses belonging to bulk traders and exporters where *Khat* is processed and readied for the market. Accordingly, its stalks are laid lengthwise and tied together into bundles of varying size after reaping. This task is usually the exclusive work domain of children and youth since they are easily controllable and their labor costs less than the average. Their employers, who cannot deny them free access to the *Khat* that is lying around as leftover, let their young workers manage their addiction to the substance in this manner, and thereby more or less permanently control and shackle them to their establishment. (See Girma Negash, 2017, for an in-depth study of the situation of these young workers).

3.2.3 Local economy and local community

Regarding the livelihood of the farmers in the rural communities surrounding the city – that are within the Harari National Regional State – are major producers of *Khat*. They have shifted from growing food crops to *Khat* cultivation, and to consuming food that they buy from the market. As a result of the shift, these farmers have come to rip significantly higher cash income, in the same measure as they have become dependent on the market for their consumption.

Most urbanites – that make up a large majority of the population of the National Regional State – are consumers of *Khat* and a few are engaged in it's marketing. There are still very few that have made good money exporting *Khat* from Aweday to Somalia.

As indicated by nearly all informants of the study, including Ato Mohamed Rahmet, Public Finance Administration Core Process Owner, and Ato Abdulbasit Abubakar, Officer for NGOs at BoFED, *Khat*'s major negative economic impact lies in that many educated young residents of the city spend their time chewing *Khat* and being economically inactive. Furthermore, *Khat*'s adverse impacts on the physical and mental health of the population develop into negative economic repercussions at the family and community levels since the latter are forced to foot the health bill of their addict members who suffer from physical and mental ill health and end up requiring medical attention sooner or later.

From 2003 to 2011, *Khat* excise tax-posts (ኬላዎች) were removed and the excise-tax was abolished because a cost-benefit assessment undertaken on it showed that the posts only delayed movement of bulk *Khat* for export. As a result municipal revenue from *Khat* tax has declined. Nowadays, retail traders that sell *Khat* in the shades are made to pay service-tax in addition to fixed income tax, which is used to cover the cost of cleaning the market area. Yet, less than 10% of all traders pay these taxes.

Ato Hailu Bekele of HIAC said the following in regard to the snowballing economic impact of *Khat* consumption:

> The negative financial impact of *Khat* consumption is tremendous. *Khat* is not consumed singularly but together with other things such as soft drinks, energy drinks, *Shisha*, and also cannabis. Moreover, as the surrounding rural community has shifted to producing *Khat*, people there have begun to eat spaghetti and macaroni bought from the market, loosing their once cherished economic self-sufficiency and independence.

The six religious leaders and community elders, participating in an FGD, lamented the fact that production of food in the region has progressively gone down so much so that food items have become too expensive. Furthermore, they expressed their disgust with the privileged position assigned to the *Khat* trade by the Government, in the following terms:

> It is said that the government collects some 2 million Birr daily in tax from the export of *Khat* from Aweday alone. A single wholesale trader, a woman by the name of Sura, who considered checkposts (ኬላዎች) to be nuisances to her trade, was behind their removal a few years back. Thus, the Government is so far solely in favor of promoting the *Khat* trade, and ought to do something about it as people are calling for regulation.

Ato Ordin Bedri, Deputy Head of the Bureau of Education of Harar NRS, and member of the Steering Committee, made the following observation on *Khat* Addiction and Prevention:

> *Khat* is an important source of income for country and farmers in the Harar area. Hence, it is quite a challenge to reduce its production thorough enforceable regulations. For the same reason it is better to teach people to reduce their consumption rather than to stop completely.

One other interesting aspect of *Khat* use that is associated with the structure of the local economy and community is its class distinctive nature. Informants were unstinting in their disclosure of the association they said to exist between patterns of *Khat* consumption and class membership. They maintained that the poor whom they invariably associated with newcomers to Harar and therefore ethnically to non-Harari, were the ones who would chew *Khat* in public places, and also the majority of the group that is in bad ways. The well-to-do, on the other hand, among whom almost all of the Harari are to be found, they claim, chew *Khat* in specifically assigned rooms at home and in a relatively disciplined manner.

3.2.4   Health and health service

Our informants in Harar were even more vehement in their disclosures of the seriousness of the impact of *Khat* on the health status the city's population, in the three areas: physical, mental, and reproductive health.

Physical health: Constipation, stomach ulcer, emaciation, skin disease, etc., are further aggravated as *Khat* that is sprayed with *Malathion* and DDT[11] has taken over the market.

---

[11] Medical science's position on the deleterious impacts of pesticides is unambiguous. It is well proven that pesticides, including Maletheon and DDT, have harmful effects on human health *ranging from short-term impacts such as headaches and nausea to chronic impacts like cancer, reproductive harm, and endocrine disruption.* A systematic review (Bassil et al, 2007) found that, "most studies on non-Hodgkin lymphoma and leukemia showed positive associations with pesticide exposure". Exposure to pesticides is also associated with non-cancerous diseases, according to Sanborn et al, who state as follows:

> Strong evidence of association with pesticide exposure was found for all neurologic outcomes, genotoxicity, and 4 of 6 reproductive effects: birth defects, fetal death, altered growth, and other outcomes. Exposure to pesticides generally doubled the level of genetic damage as measured by chromosome aberrations in lymphocytes... (Sanborn et al, 2007: 1712).

Ato Tekalegn Mehari, a long-time resident of Harar and Dire-Dawa, and a teacher, provided his observation concerning the linkage between *Khat* chewing and physical health:

> Many heavy *Khat* chewers or addicts suffer from constipation particularly in the morning due to the forage that enters their digestive system little by little, and accumulates undigested inside the intestine blocking normal defecation. Such people habitually take an early morning serving of *Khat* that is locally known as *Udu banna* (bottom opener) in order to activate their system and be able to relieve themselves. When the problem gets too serous, they make use of laxatives. Hence, due to the wide spread consumption of *Khat*, there is no place in the country where various types of laxatives and sedatives are sold by pharmacies as much as in Harar. It is noteworthy that both of these substances are to be found nearly in every *Khat* consumer's home. (See Subsection 2.2.4 for the standpoint of the medical science literature, which is generally in agreement with the statements in this paragraph).
>
> Heavy *Khat* chewers or addicts are also unable to even get out of their beds without chewing some *Khat*. Their bodily system remains shut down, and they are unable to accomplish even the most basic every-day duty unless it is reactivated with an early serving of a small amount of *Khat* that is known as *Ijja bana* (eye opener).
>
> Such persons also suffer from *Dukak* whenever they go to bed without having their fill of *Khat*. The terrible mental suffering they experience under *Dukak* is unbearable to them and the people who share their bedrooms.

Nowadays, *Khat* growers regularly spray their plantations with a type of pesticide, *Malathion,* in order to render their produce shiny and attractive to buyers. Farmers claim that this posses no danger to the health of chewers as the chemical is easily washed away by rainwater, and some doctors too advise patients to wash their *Khat* with water before consuming it. But, neither of these does nothing and the *Malathion* causes serious health hazard that is not less than *Khat* addiction, such as stomach disease —according to informants who dwelt on the subject.

Prenatal and childhood exposure to pesticides was also found to be associated with impairments in neurobehavioral in later life by epidemiological studies reviewed by Jurewicz and Hanke (2008: 121).

All six participants in the FGD of religious leaders and community elders agreed in pointing out that,

> A more serious problem has appeared these days, namely that of *Khat* treated with *Malathion* and DDT has surfaced. Already, some 6-8 people are known to have died from chewing *Khat* that is tainted with these chemicals. *Khat* leads to addiction to smoking tobacco, *Shisha*, and even cannabis, all of which are sources of serious physical and mental health hazard in the long run.

Ato Afendi Bashi, who, being the Deputy Director of the Health Bureau, was in a position to know, lend support to the foregoing assessment, when he said, "*Khat* growers have started spraying the anti-malaria spray to make their product appear more attractive to buyers".

A couple of informants also raise the implication that the above-described practice of treating *Khat* plants with chemicals has for future generations. They were apprehensive of the looming danger that pesticides and anti-malaria sprays pose for the children of chewers of the tainted *Khat*. (See footnote No. 7, on the foregoing page, for the position of medical science on this).

The single important physical disorder that was, surprisingly, not mentioned by the study informants, but the widespread existence of which was confirmed time and again through the observation of the study team in the course of the field work in Harar, was oral decay. Many elderly persons and some young ones were seen with their small *Muqächa*, either carrying them or in the process of using them to pound *Khat* into mush that can be easily imbibed. What was surprising to the field team was to see young men with no gray hair on their head to be among the mashed *Khat* consumers, having already lost their teeth to oral decay that has set in very early.

Mental health: Mental health-care providers speak of insomnia, depression psychosis and others as being associated with *Khat*, since most mental patients that chew the substance exhibit these ailments or their symptoms. Thus, *Khat* is at least an aggravating factor, if not an outright cause, of mental illness in Harar and the surrounding areas. (See Subsection 2.2.4 for the standpoint of the medical science literature, which is generally in agreement with the statements contained in this paragraph).

One of the peculiarities of Harar City that jumps to the eye of any casual or expert observer is definitely the unusually large number of mentally deranged persons. Ato Abdulaziz Mohammad, Youth and Women Mainstreaming and Projects Coordination Process Owner, BoWYCA, shared his observation on this subject:

> If you go out to the street now you will not walk for 50 meters before coming across a mentally ill person with *Khat* in his hand. The presence of the mentally ill is so overwhelming. I believe that the Emmanuel Psychiatric Hospital in Addis Ababa should have been located here in Harar.

The impact of *Khat* abuse on the mental health of people in Harar does not stop at getting them committed to psychiatric institutions; it accompanies them on the inside to disrupt and reverse the little psychiatric treatment that is given to them while they are there. Ato Habtamu Tadesse (BSc in Psychiatry working as Physician and Nurse) and Wz. Aster Mulugeta (BSc in Clinical Nursing and Diploma in Psychiatry) staff of the Department of Psychiatry of Hiwot Fana Specialized University Hospital, jointly shared the following on the Psychiatric Ward and their patients:

> The main cause of mental ill health in this city is *Khat* followed by *Shisha*, cigarette and *Ganja* [cannabis]. All of our patients are *Khat* addicts and abusers. *Khat* is definitely an aggravating factor, if not a cause, of mental illness in Harar and the surrounding areas. Those that are from the urban section of Harar are multiple substance users, namely that of *Khat*, *Shisha*, *Ganja*, as well as tobacco, alcohol and glue.

> All patients in the psychiatric ward are *Khat* addicts and abusers, and because of their continued use of *Khat* even when they are in the hospital, they go without sleep and this worsens their condition. Whatever curative treatment we give to our patents, it is impeded by their chewing of *Khat* while under treatment. The patients that come to us are psychotic, in depression, bipolar or schizophrenic. They could also have one or two of these. Since most of them are psychotic, they use the sedative medication we give them as *Č'äbsi* substance [i.e., in lieu of alcohol used to break *Khat* highs].

> There are many more mentally sick persons in the streets of Harar as compared to any other town in the country. Moreover, the number of the mentally ill in the city appears to be growing.

As for the mental health care that is available, the only institution that is currently in existence in the city is the University Hospital's Psychiatric Ward, but it is a psychiatric ward only in name, as it lacks practically everything from health professionals to medication, etc.

It ought to be noted that the above mentioned University Hospital's Psychiatric Ward caters to the mentally ill in general, and does not undertake any particular treatment or rehabilitation of substance abusers, including *Khat* addicts. Ato Selamyehun Aklilu, Director of Stand for Integrated Development - Ethiopia (SID-E), said the following concerning this limitation in health service provision in the city, with an obvious feeling of desperation:

> In the old days, there was a lunatic asylum (እብድ ቤት) in the city to which mentally ill *Khat* addicts used to be confined. Nowadays, there are no such places of confinement or rehabilitation for *Khat* addicts, and therefore the mentally ill addicts go around picking *Khat Gäraba* to satisfy their addiction. In their desperation, they pose danger to others as well as themselves, and some even go to the extent of committing suicide.

Abdulwassi of HIAC was of the opinion that, "*Khat* has caused mental illnesses to quite a lot of people, whom one sees walking the streets *and* competing with goats for discarded *Khat Gäraba*.

Reproductive health and impotence: Ex-addicts, and sex-workers report very low concern for sex and inability to perform by men who chew *Khat*. As one of the three participants of the ex-addicts FGD stated, heavy use of *Khat* leads to impotence and divorce. (ጫት ስንፈተ-ወሲብ በወንድ ላይ በማስከተል ለፍች ይዳርጋል። እኔ ጫትን እንጅ የሴቱን ነገር ጉዳዮም አልለውም ነበር።) This view was supported by one of the participants in the religious leaders and community elders FGD, who said:

> *Khat* is also known to weaken the sexual performance of men leading to divorce and family dissolution. This is the most serious problem with *Khat* chewing, because it makes the man sexually zero! (For the position of medical science on the effects of *Khat* on human health in general and reproductive health in particular, see the description at the end of Subsection 2.2.4).

Ato H of HIAC gave an honest testimony based on his own personal experience when he said, "I myself used to chew *Khat* and have experienced problems including that of impotence".

Ato Tariku Duressa, Vice-President of Harari NRS Supreme Court, explained how the role of impotence in many divorce cases is somewhat disguised, when he observed,

> *Khat* is leading to sexual impotence, and it is behind many divorce cases that the Court deals with, although the Revised Family Law does not require a plaintive to disclose the cause for the request to divorce.

Finally, Ato Sissay Dereje, Study, Drafting and Training Core Process Owner at the Bureau of Justice and Security shared his bleak view of the health situation in Harar, and dismissing the single often mentioned "positive social impact of *Khat*" as untenable:

> *Khat* addiction is a sickness since it makes people not operate in their right minds. Pesticides and anti-malaria sprays the effect of which can be inherited by the children of those who chew tainted *Khat* is our serious worry today. The only positive thing that can be said about *Khat* is its contribution towards social facilitation at the initial stage of the chewing sessions. But, even that is short-lived, since chewers become self-absorbed once they have attained *Märqana*.

The finding of medical science on the subject of the impact of *Khat* on human health in general and reproductive health in particular, is by and large in agreement with what has been learnt from this study's informants. For the conclusions reflected in the scientific literature, the reader is advised to refer to the brief presentation already given under Subsection 2.2.4.

3.2.5   Education and educational institutions

Whereas *Khat* impacts educational institutions and those closely associated with them in general, it has very special close relationship with tertiary level ones. Hence, this section presents the findings of the study regarding the impacts of *Khat* on education and educational institutions in Harar City, first, in general, and then, as it pertains to the tertiary level in particular.

3.2.5.1   *Education and educational institutions in general*

Students who chew *Khat* are more likely to come late to class, drop out of school, avoid going to the library, and be isolated. *Khat* addicted parents are often very careless and do not follow up their children's education even registering them. Many school-aged children who have dropped out of school and are engaged in *Khat* trade, particularly in Dire Teyara area.

Many teachers chew *Khat*, and those that are addicted to it underperform, as they skip classes, come late, and are temperamental. Most *Khat*-chewing teachers also drink alcohol to 'break' the *Khat* high, as well as smoking tobacco and *Shisha*. All of these indulgencies push their expenditure beyond what their salaries could cover throwing them and their families into deep economic hardship and crisis. The majority of teachers who chew *Khat* do not accomplish their tasks properly, although there are few that consume *Khat* with discipline and do their job fairly well

Informants also cite the problem with *Khat* lies in that there are a number of attendants to it, including *Shisha*, alcohol, etc. *Khat* even leads to cannabis addiction. It costs a lot and therefore becomes a source of family conflict. I myself [Ato Teshome] used to chew *Khat* regularly, and I needed to chew *Khat* daily in order to perform my duties as a teacher

Ato Ordin Bedri, Deputy Head of the BoE and member of the Steering Committee on *Khat* Addiction and Prevention, supplied the following statement that deserves to be quoted at length:

> My personal opinion on *Khat* is as follows: (1) it has detrimental impact on the economy of individuals that chew it, sometimes leading them into criminal acts such as theft (2) there are also adverse health impacts such as mental illness (3) depending on how often and how much *Khat* they consume, it is possible for some to use it to stay at home and read.

> As for its impact on education, students who chew *Khat* are more likely to come late to class, to drop out of school, etc. Also, they don't go to the library, and don't create network with others. In general, the adverse impacts of *Khat* clearly outweigh the positive ones. It also affects the children's access to education as *Khat* addicted parents are often very careless and neglect children. Such parents do not follow up their children's education say by even registering them. There are also many

school-aged children who have dropped out of school and are engaged in *Khat* trade.

Many teachers chew *Khat*. Those who are addicts underperform, as they skip classes, come late, and are temperamental. A lot of them drink alcohol to 'break' the *Khat* high. But there are some that consume *Khat* with discipline and do their job fairly well. But, the majority of teachers who chew *Khat* do not accomplish their tasks properly, and this is true for other civil servants as well.

Khat chewing has negative economic impact on teachers, as their salary is not sufficient for them to cover their living expenses and the cost of their *Khat* consumption. There are teachers that also drink alcohol *Č'äbsi* (in order to break the effect of the *Khat* high) as well as smoking *Shisha* —indulgences that push their expenditure high up.

We have student ethics and civics clubs in all schools, and we try to use the mass media to serve these clubs. But, unfortunately we do not have similar activity for teachers. Our efforts in this regard are limited and not at all sufficient.

Disciplinary measures are taken against teachers for repeated absence, but not for chewing *Khat,* as the latter is not illegal. Also, disciplinary actions are taken against teachers, for failure of duty such as absenteeism without investigating the causes behind the failures that could include addiction.

Parents regularly give money to their children to buy *Khat* and also provide them with rooms dedicated to *Khat* chewing at home. This is done with the intention of keeping the children at home and away from the streets, but it only facilitates the regular chewing of *Khat*.

Since students in the universities, TVETS, and training colleges live together in large numbers, the situation is conductive for peer pressure to facilitate the spread of *Khat* chewing. As for Haromaya University, *Khat* is easily available there since it is located in a rural area that grows *Khat* in abundance.

The only organized response to combat *Khat* addiction in schools is limited to mini-media and civic and ethics clubs that give advice to students not to chew *Khat*. These are, however, voluntary activities and separate from the One-in-Five Educational Development Army. The ethics and civics clubs are not active, either. Moreover, such intervention work ought to start at the family level, since many parents give their children money for the purchase of *Khat* and it is common for children to be seen chewing it in front of their parents. Some parents do this to keep their children close to them at home, but it is counterproductive from the point of combating *Khat* addiction among the youth in general and school-age children in particular.

Regarding the prevalence of *Khat* chewers among students of 1st to 12th grade, the following are my estimates:

> Girls: less then 1%, as they get into *Khat* chewing after marriage
>
> Boys: about 5%.

I believe it is possible to reverse the *Khat* situation, as we have managed to address other matters that were considered impossible. We need decisive and sustained measures. Thinking of only Harar City, I believe that there is a reversal of the earlier trend concerning the attitude of people towards *Khat*.

It is not much that can be done by way of regulation in places that are already under the spread of *Khat* such as Harar. Here in Harar, what can be done is the creation of awareness to make people give up or reduce their consummation of *Khat*. On the contrary, in places where *Khat* is being newly introduced, it could be possible to use regulation to restrict its spread.

Ato Henok Tedla, a 26-year old heavy *Khat* addict, said that it was his addiction that negatively affected his education. When he was in high school he used to take powdered *Khat* to school, as he was unable to sit in class unless he keeps on chewing *Khat*. He finally dropped out of school as *Khat* addiction took over him completely to the extent that he could not keep up his attendance and abide by the rest of the school regulations.

Ato Mohamed Rahmet, Public Finance Administration Core Process Owner, and Ato Abdulbasit Abubakar, Officer for NGOs at BoFED, were in agreement that, *"Khat's* major negative economic impact lies in that many educated young residents of the city spend their time chewing *Khat* and being economically inactive".

3.2.5.2 Tertiary-level education and educational institutions

Since students in the universities, colleges and TVETs, live together in large numbers, the situation is conducive for peer pressure to facilitate the spread of *Khat* chewing and addiction. Some one-third of the students at College of Health and Medical Science, Haromaya University, Harar Campus chew *Khat* regularly or daily; and according to a police report, the students who chew *Khat* also smoke cannabis and some have been penalized having been caught in its possession. Students at Haromaya University are major consumers of *Khat*, and they have made the University a conduit for the supply of cannabis. There are *Khat*-chewing students that have dropped out due to health problems, particularly mental ill health.

Student Abdu Ibrahim, Student Council President of College of Health and Medical Science, Haromaya University, Harar Campus, gave the following lengthy description of the prevalence impacts of *Khat* and at that institute:

> The total population of the campus is 2,500 students plus the academic and support staff of the College. Some 35% of the students chew *Khat* regularly or daily. Those from Hararge region do not study without chewing *Khat*; and most of them do not use other substances and also do not use it continuously once exams are over. *Khat* chewing is quite common amongst Ethiopian Somali student (numbering 110) and Oromo students some of whom are from Hararge region (numbering 997-1100 in total).

> There are some among the girl students, making up 34% of the student population, who chew *Khat*. But, such girls make up a small minority because control in the girls' dormitory is stricter. The other reason for only few girls to be *Khat* chewers is their fear of acquiring negative reputation that can tarnish their later life.

> The fact that the study/work load on students of the Health and Medical Science Faculty is heavy, pushes students to use *Khat* for staying awake and concentrating on what they read.

> The police tell us that students who chew *Khat* also tend to smoke cannabis. We have even bailed out some students who had been caught smoking cannabis from jail at the police station. The majority of students are vulnerable to acquiring such habits, due to the location of the campus inside the city leading to the easy availability of addictive substances.

There are students that have been punished for smoking cannabis on campus. Whenever we conducted searches of the dormitories, we have found cannabis and cannabis smoking equipments. As for *Shisha*, it is smoked outside of the campus in *Shisha* bars.

Our records show that there are students who chew *Khat* but who do not smoke cannabis or *Shisha*. But all students who smoke cannabis and *Shisha* also chew *Khat* regularly. Some students that I have talked to told me that drinking alcohol induces them to smoke cigarettes.

Disciplinary measures are taken according to the provisions of the Code of Conduct of Haramaya University that does not cover students' behavior and action outside of the campus walls. Therefore, students are free to do as they please outside of the campus regarding drugs.

The university does not currently have sufficiently strict and applied rules regarding drugs. Students can get around the rule against bringing in *Khat* into the campus by bribing or begging the campus guards to look the other way. Other times, students throw their bundles of *Khat* over the fence of the campus to their friends who wait to pick it from the inside, or for them to pick it up later on. Thus, students manage to get their way with *Khat* consumption inside campus, contrary to what is stipulated in the Code of Conduct.

Most of the *Khat*-chewing students have limited social life. They are usually lonely, and are seen just sitting or studying by themselves. They do not take shower or wash their clothes regularly. They do not attend class regularly either.

There are *Khat*-chewing students that quit their study due to health problems, particularly mental ill health. But it is not possible to trace their mental health problems directly to *Khat* with absolute certainty. Further study is required to establish the direction and strength of the causal relationship.

The above call for further research concerning the causal linkage between *Khat* chewing and mental suffering among Haromaya University's Harar Campus students, is well taken. The scientific literature, too, points out that the chemical mechanism through which *Khat* affects the mind is still not conclusively known, the same way whether addiction to *Khat* is only social or also physiological. However, it ought to be mentioned that scientific research that have been undertaken on the contribution of *Khat* to mental illness among Ethiopian university students, including those of

Haromaya University, are helping to deal away with such lingering doubts. Thus, a cross-sectional survey carried out on mental distress among Ethiopian university students in 2012/13 by three medical and public health faculty members of Haromaya University in Harar and Gonder University, has arrived at the following major conclusions:

> About one fifth (21.6 %) of the university students had mental distress. The likelihood of having mental distress were higher among students who had family history of mental illness, never attended religious programs, frequent conflicts with their fellows and chew *Khat* (Yadeta Dessie *et al*, 2013: 4).

The FGD of six religious leaders and community elders underlined the close linkage between university education and substance abuse, including that of *Khat*, as follows:

> If you check out the situation at Haromaya University, you will learn that *Khat* chewing, as well as *Shisha*, tobacco and cannabis smoking are wide spread, which is not due to lack of employment as all are either students, teachers or support staff.

Ato Tekalegn Mehari, a long-time teacher, lent his support by saying, "Students at Haromaya University are major consumers of *Khat*, and they have made the University a transit for the cannabis trade".

3.2.6   Crime and correction

The findings of the study in this respect, indicate that, whereas *Khat* induced domestic sexual abuse and *Khat* related petty property crime committed within the family are common in Harar, theft outside the family or in public places is rare because people who chew *Khat* are too dormant and fearful of strangers. Cannabis smoking – which is illegal – following the chewing of *Khat,* is becoming common, as are cases of growing and marketing it.

Ato Tariku Duressa, Vice-President of Harari NRS Supreme Court, describes his observation from the bench as follows:

> Most criminal cases that appear before the High Court in Harar concern domestic abuses, fights, and rapes that are fuelled by *Khat*. ...

> Theft that is committed outside the family is not widespread, because people who chew *Khat* are too fearful and scared to commit theft [on the

property of strangers].[12] Also, people here are not in the habit of going after each other's wives.

Cannabis, which is usually smoked following *Khat* chewing, is becoming common. Not only the smoking of cannabis, but even growing it is spreading. Most of the case that come to the Court concern cannabis consumers. Cannabis is becoming a business – both of its production/growing and marketing. I am afraid that cannabis consumption is going to spread beyond university and high school students, to elementary students. There are also many divorce cases, most of which are related to *Khat* and attendant substance consumption by one or the other of the parties.

Ato Sissay Dereje, Study, Drafting and Training Core Process Owner at the Bureau of Justice and Security expressed his measured opinion on the state of crime in the Regional State, both its rural and urban sections, as follows:

Khat stealing is rare. But, there are some individuals who steal *Khat* from the plantation of other farmers that are derogatorily labeled *Aba Č'äbsi (Khat* plant breakers). I have heard the story of one such *Aba Č'äbsi* whose hands were cut off and sent away [back to his home village] together with the *Khat* bundles that he had stolen as a kind of warning to others. Generally speaking, people in Harar are friendly and peaceful to the extent that theft on streets is rare.

Deputy-Inspector Yasin Shukri, Community Policing Process Owner of Harari NRS, expressed his views on the relationship of *Khat*, abuse of attendant substances, individual aggression, and crime, in the following terms:

People are caught within some five vicious cycles as a result of their *Khat* abuse: 1. Some do not respect the agreements they have entered 2. Others become extremely suspicious of others including their wives' integrity 3. Still others do not attend to their tasks and responsibilities 4. Because everything is simple and easy for those that chew *Khat*, they do not take care of their personal hygiene, etc. 5. As their income is not enough to cover their expenses, they are pushed into all sorts of corruption and criminal activity.

---

[12] Contrary to this statement, the medical literature indicates that *Khat* consumption is associated with aggressive, anti-social and criminal behaviors. (Banjaw et al, 2006; Philpart et al, 2009; Odenwald *et al*, 2008; Alem and Shibre, 1997).

Being under the influence of *Khat* makes people inactive or dormant, let alone be capable of committing theft. But it should be realized that the *Khat* chewer is not the same person under different circumstances and at different times of the day: he is different early in the day when he is experiencing *Harara* (acute *Khat* hunger), then later in the day when after chewing sufficient amounts and is in high on *Khat*, and finally after breaking the *Märqana* with alcohol or some other activity of *Č'äbsi*.

There are members of the police force who were dismissed form the force due to their frequent absence from work resulting from their *Khat* addiction. *Khat* has even made its way into prison and guards who sell it to inmates. People seem to be receptive of anti-*Khat* messages recently. A policeman once said that they guard prisoners by giving them *Khat*, since they become docile and manageable once they get their *Khat* fill.

Ato Hailu Bekele of HIAC related a story regarding the contribution of *Khat* to criminal behavior, which follows:

A young *Khat* addicted male who lived with his grandmother kept selling household stuff such as blankets to finance his *Khat* habit, when he run out of items to sell, he fought his grandmother as he now wanted to dismantle and sell off the corrugated iron covering the roof of his side of the house, as he put it, that he shared with the grandmother.

The reference to incestuous rape being performed under *Khat* intoxication that is made both in the foregoing page (as well as in Subsection 3.3.2), on the one hand, and the contention that long-term *Khat* consumption is associated with erectile dysfunction and impotence that is made elsewhere, on the other, appear to be contradictory. This seeming paradox is not only noteworthy, but also begs for clarification. The explanation for this is very simple. As much as it is true that all adult males are definitely not all long-term *Khat* consumers, the probability that there will always be individuals who are *Khat* intoxicated, and therefore sexually motivated and temporarily while being free of inhibition to take advantage of the opportunity the privacy of the family hearth provides. In brief, the two impacts of *Khat* while mutually exclusive at the individual level, they are, if not supplementary, coexistent at the societal level.

3.2.7   Civil service delivery

The findings of the study on the impact of *Khat* on governance are loud and clear, and cover three distinct areas of governance failure. Absenteeism, tardiness, underperformance and corruption were the focus of the unsolicited information obtained from both ordinary residents and government officials on the subject.

Khat negatively affects the performance of civil servants in all walks of administration. Some do not work at all in the afternoons. Others are incapable off making the right kind of decision while under the influence of *Khat*, since a *Khat* dependent person is always negative when he has not chewed his *Khat*, and very positive and too accommodating when he has had his fill.

Religious leaders and community elders informing this study were adamant that, nowadays, almost all civil servants chew *Khat* and some are even led into other related habits including that of *Shisha* and cannabis smoking, which raises their expenses and lead them to corruption.

Khat chewing is so widespread among civil servants that people advice those that seek their services not to go to certain officials in the morning – i.e., before they have chewed their daily *Khat*. *Khat* dependent government employees make use of such practices as *lightening* that is also known as *instant Bärč'a*, and *Atterera* (አጥባራራ) to get around office rules that bar them from abandoning their work station for long durations or openly consuming *Khat* right there.

Ato Tekalegn Mehari, the long-time resident of Harar and Dire-Dawa, and a teacher by profession, explains the details of the mechanisms that are employed by civil servants to get around regulations prohibiting the consumption of *Khat* at the workplace:

> Civil servants commonly resort to what are known as *Atterera* (አጥባራራ) and *Lightening* (ላይትኒንግ) in order to consume *Khat* at their work places without openly break its prohibition. *Atterera* is a term referring to a bunch of *Khat* buds that are nipped and kept from sight to be consumed hastily in emergency situations, i.e., situations that do not permit the elaborate ceremony due to shortage of time. *Lightening* is a term obviously borrowed from English to refer to a quick *Khat* consumption that takes only some 30 minutes. Also known as *instant Bärč'a*, the format is very popular among government employees as it fits well within their short lunch and coffee breaks.

Ato Abdulwassi, of HIAC, added, "Many office workers are observed rushing to complete their *lightening* sessions and get back to the office in the middle of the day".

Ato Muktar, Director of EYNHB, shared the extreme cat-and-mice game that was played by rogue civil servants and the public:

> Tardiness and absenteeism due to *Khat* addiction are widespread practices of civil servants. As a result, the Regional Government was at one time forced to introduce fingerprint scanning in offices for recording attendance, but this failed to produce its intended outcome as many of the civil servants promptly went back home after signing in. Then, some members of the public who absolutely needed the services of the rogue government workers tried to catch them at the fingerprint stations trying to be served right there before the former could disappear again.

Wz. Sarah Mohammad, EYNHB Officer, added:

> The problem of civil servant absenteeism from office is so widespread that people advise you not to go to certain officials in the morning before they have chewed their daily *Khat* —because they would be in a bad mood and hence disposed to be dismissive or negative towards clients. To approach them in the afternoon after they have had their fill would be the right thing to do.

Ato Tariku Duressa, Vice-President of Harari NRS Supreme Court, frankly admitted that, "*Khat* chewing is negatively impacting office work. Even here at the Supreme Court, very few workers are present at their workstation at certain times of the working day".

Another detrimental impact of *Khat* on civil service delivery lies in its contribution towards corruption (as the income of civil servants is not sufficient to cover their *Khat* and related expenses), and there is nothing done by the government in this regard.

Ato Sissay Dereje, Study, Drafting and Training Core Process Owner at the Bureau of Justice and Security, noted:

> Concerning *Khat* and ethics, people do not respect ethical guidelines while under the influence of *Khat*. They are not truthful. They are not fair, as they favor and side with those who share their own types. There are government officials who do not come to office in the afternoon due to their dependence on *Khat*. Even having given appointments to several service seekers, they fail to show up.

Vice-Inspector Yasin Shukri, Community Policing Process Owner of Harari NRS, remarked on the situation in his work domain:

> There are members of the police force who were dismissed form the force due to their frequent absence from work due to their *Khat* addiction. *Khat* has even made its way into prisons and prison wardens who sell it to inmates. A prison warden once said that they handle prisoners more efficiently by allowing them to obtain *Khat*, since they become docile and manageable once they get their *Khat* fill.

3.2.8   Concerning *Khat's* positive impacts – or the lack of them – in Harar

The same way the study's data collection activities were conducted in Assosa, attempts were made in Harar to learn from informants about possible positive impacts of *Khat* on the city and its population. Here too, as informants did not come up spontaneously with any positive socioeconomic impacts of *Khat*, they were prodded by being asked pointedly and repeatedly for any for any benefits that could be had by chewing the substance. In this manner, two benefits of *Khat* were elicited from few informants; namely, *social facilitation* (Pantelis *et al*, 1989: 659; Kennedy, 1987). But the same informants qualified even these benefits, saying the *social facilitation* effect is only temporary and lasts only until the chewers in the group get high becoming self-absorbed. Thus, instead of *social facilitation* the consumption of *Khat* actually curtails social life.

A second effect of *Khat*, that is presumed to be beneficial by a couple of the study informants, namely its attribute of *warding off sleep during nightlong prayer vigils*. But the same informants went on to qualify their statements by arguing in the same breath, that even this was something that is used by some regular chewers as an excuse to be supplied with abundant *Khat*. So also, informants of this study did not at all mention *the suppression of appetite/hunger* that is considered to be another beneficial effect of the consumption of *Khat* by some writers (Lemieux *et al*, 2014).

There is yet a third attribute of *Khat* that is considered to be positive and significant enough to be behind its popular use among manual laborers and students. This concerns its capacity to subdue fatigue and relieve pain caused by arduous work of long duration that involves repetitive tasks or intense concentration. This was attested by some of the study informants and supported by the findings of other field researchers such as John Kennedy who undertook a similar investigation on the use of *Khat* in North Yemen (Kennedy 1987: 79, 122).

However, some informants of this study have added that the above-mentioned function of *Khat* in reducing pain and fatigue comes with a price. Since *Khat* allows chewers to tolerate pain and tiredness and thus exert themselves at work beyond the natural tolerance threshold of their body over a long period of abuse, it leads to the overstraining of their systems and premature aging -a phenomenon they refer to as "early burning-out".

Furthermore, the same function of *Khat* in facilitating the tolerance of work fatigue and intense concentration comes with a large price tag at the societal level. One study has, thus, brought to light an interesting finding showing how widespread consumption of *Khat* across the country leads to wastage of time. It has revealed that about 297 million *Khat* chewing sessions take place every year in Ethiopia (Gessesse Dessie, 2013).

It is also noteworthy, that in Harar, as in Assosa, informants in Harar did not raise either the issue of tooth decay and oral cavity problems, which they probably thought of as too obvious to deserve mention. The same is true of the adverse impacts of *Khat* on pregnant and lactating women, which very few informants in Harar mentioned only in general terms, probably because they are not aware of their mechanisms to properly articulate them.

Finally, before living the issue of socioeconomic impacts at this point, a brief reminder, which concerns the interconnectedness of the various impacts described in the foregoing sections, needs to be made. While these impacts of *Khat* in the various domains of the social arena had to be differentiated and treated as such for analytical purposes, it is equally important to recognize the fact that they are interrelated and that their cumulative impact is more than just the sum of the individual entities. Obviously, this statement applies for the socioeconomic impacts *Khat* in Assosa as it does for those in Harar.

3.3 Measures Underway in Harar to Curb the Escalating *Khat* Consumption & Addiction, and Rehabilitate Addicts

3.3.1 Measures undertaken by governmental organizations

Government action to counteract the spread of *Khat* consumption an addiction is conspicuous, if for anything, only for its virtual absence. From policy, to practical impeding measures and to treatment and rehabilitation, all are areas of intervention for which the government can be blamed for omission. The only fledgling effort that the regional government has made so far, relates to giving support to the awareness creation movement that is initiated and spearheaded by a consortium of civil society organizations, through its formal leadership of the Steering Committee on *Khat* Addiction and Prevention – which is the subject of the next Subsection.

Ato Abdulaziz Mohammad, Youth and Women Mainstreaming and Projects Coordination Process Owner, BoWCYA, after frankly admitting that the Bureau has not conducted any study on *Khat* so far and what he was saying was mainly based on his personal observation and experience, shared the information that follows:

> The 2010 EDHS puts Harar as the primary *Khat*-consuming city. We, also, have observed that the *Khat* problem is both widespread and serious in the City of Harar. Hence, the following limited measures have been taken, to date: (1) Since *Khat* chewing is encouraged by unemployment, we as a government have provided credit for micro and small enterprises in order to create employment for the young (2) Some sports facilities and gyms are built to provide the youth with alternative leisure-time activities (3) Youth centers, too, are built, and (4) Community conversation is started to make people aware of the problem associated with *Khat* and its attendant substances.

> Yet, the effort to address the problem of *Khat* chewing has remained limited. Thus: (1) In spite of the widespread occurrence of mental illness in the city, there is no proper psychiatric hospital or facility in Harar (2) More of all the measures that are begun and listed above ought to be further strengthened or expanded.

> The NGO efforts to curtail the spread of *Khat* are supported by our Bureau of Women, Youth and Children Affairs, as the NGOs operate on the basis of a tripartite agreement between the regional BoFED, our BoWCYA and the respective NGOs. Furthermore, our Bureau is a member of the Steering Committee set up by the regional bureaus and some NGOs for the purpose of curbing the spread of *Khat*.

> I believe that we cannot ban *Khat* chewing or preach to people to totally quit their *Khat* chewing habits. We should rather tell people to limit their consumption of *Khat* or control their consumption of *Khat* instead of being controlled by it. In other words, we should advise people to limit themselves to becoming social chewers. Otherwise, people will consider us a bunch of hypocrites, since they know very well that we will go to chewing *Khat* right after saying those things at the awareness meeting.

Khalid Anwar, Advisor on Social Affairs at the Regional President's Office was equally frank regarding the limitation of government intervention, and said:

> We do not have a specific program on *Khat* as a government. But we have 'Youth Health' as one of the 15 urban development issues we work on. We also make effort to close down *Shisha* houses.

The only direct activity that is underway in order to deal with the escalating *Khat* consumption and addiction is the one that is sponsored by CSSP and implemented by local CSOs. Yet, even this is only at its initial stage.

The solution in restricting the spread of *Khat* should not consist of immediately jumping to take regulatory measures. It ought to be preceded by the following steps:

- Awareness creation
- Providing the farmers with substitute crops such as apples
- Look for alternative income generation activities for those engaged in *Khat* trade
- Formulate appropriate policy that is based on research informed knowledge.
- Working out a policy and action model, on the basis of research findings, to offset the enablers of the spread of *Khat* consumption and addiction, such as:
  - Peer-group pressure as well as cultural and traditional practices
  - Cheap and easy availability of *Khat* that can be dealt with by making the sale and buying of *Khat* as difficult as possible through the introduction of heavy tax.

3.3.2   Measures undertaken by civil society organizations

3.3.2.1   *The setup*

A group of civil society organizations have come together to fight back the galloping spread of *Khat* consumption and addiction under the banner of saving the future generation. Civil Society Support Program (CSSP) Eastern Regional Business Unit's Strategic Partnership Grant (SPG) (that has developed a framework for SPG 5, i.e., Control/Reduction of *Khat* Addiction and its Compliments Program, and communicated it through CSSP Western Regional Business Unit to BGDAN, and through CSSP Central Regional Business Unit to OPRIFS) is the source of financial and technical support of the initiative. The following civil society organizations are the recipient of the CSSP support and main implementers of the program in Harar:

1. Ethiopian Youth Network – Harari Branch (EYNHB) that works on the youth as the lead-grantee

2. Harari *Ïddïr* and *Afosha* Coalition (HIAC) that works with adults as a sub-grantee receiving grant and technical support from CSSP Eastern Regional Business Unit Strategic Partnership Grantees of SPG 5 to run the Control/Reduction of Addiction to *Khat* and its Compliments Program, and

3. Stand for Integrated Development-Ethiopia (SID-E) that works through five implementing agencies receiving program grant from CSSP that has also brought it together with the above two since it works on the same *Khat* related issues

Through the catalytic action of EYNHB a regional *Steering Committee on Khat Addiction and Prevention* has been set up at the regional level, with sub-committees in all of the nine *Wärädä* of the Region, in order to deal with the spread of *Khat* abuse and addiction, although it had not yet begun to function having met only once by the time of the fieldwork informing this study. Its members are:

1. The Region's President Office   -- Chair
2. Education Bureau   -- Vice Chair
3. Health Bureau   -- Member
4. Bureau of Women, Children and Youth Aff. -- Member
5. Justice Bureau   -- Member
6. Police   -- Member
7. Sports Commission   -- Member
8. Youth Federation   -- Member

Under it, the Steering Committee has set up sub-committees in all of the nine *Wärädä* of the Region.

3.3.2.2 *Measures undertaken*

Ethiopian Youth Network–Harari Branch (EYNHB) has made an important contribution by playing the catalytic role in establishing the following in order to help implement the program:

- A regional steering committee
- Steering committees at the *Wäräda* level and
- Task-force committees in youth associations.

Moreover, it has also undertaken awareness creation meetings for sex-workers, and had plans to work in schools on preventing and reducing *Khat*, at the time of the fieldwork informing this study.

Harari *Ïddïr* and *Afosha* Coalition (HIAC), a coalition of 97 Christian *Ïddïr* and Moslem *Afosha* focuses on reducing *Khat* consumption by working on and preventing new entrants from joining in. It targets and work on saving the new generation, namely children and those who are "on-and-off" or infrequent *Khat* users (ወጣ ገባ በሚሉት ላይ).

The following are the major activities undertaken by HIAC in getting started with its work, so far:

- Sensitization of the leaders of the 97 *Ïddïr* and *Afosha*, as well as religious leaders was conducted
- Five *Ïddïr* and five *Afosha* were selected, and 10 promoters/facilitators from each of these 10 *Ïddïr* and *Afosha* have conducted awareness raising discussion on issues of *Khat* abuse and addiction for the last five months, and
- Staffs of HIAC have supervised the discussions in the 10 *Ïddïr* and *Afosha*.

HIAC has also conducted a sensitization drive to make parents give up the practice of supporting their grown-up children's *Khat* habit by providing them with special pocket money and rooms.

In addition to the foregoing, HIAC has accomplished the following with support from government organizations such as the Region's Supreme Court:

- Given awareness raising training to community leaders, women, community policing officers
- Selected and trained "advocates" drawn from *Ïddïr* and *Afosha* who conduct Community Conversations on the harms of *Khat* every Sunday
- Purchased a 7-month airtime on a local radio station to run an educational program on *Khat* for its continued assistance
- Trained 45 *Khat* addict youths in security and gypsum work

- Trained 50 *Aräqe bet* operators, with plans to link them with colleges in the city so that they can work as laundry women washing students' cloths, and
- Another group was being trained at the Police Station in Community Policing, at the time of the fieldwork informing this study.

Stand for Integrated Development–Ethiopia (SID-E), together with five implementing local organizations works on some 12,000 youth. It has, among others, carried out the following:

- Worked on the provision of employment for the youth in general, and for *Khat* and related substance abuse victims in particular, by organizing them in micro and small enterprises (although the latter has not produced its expected results, one of the reasons the dependence of the candidate on *Khat* and related substances).
- Provided financial support in the form of revolving fund to 250 youth organized in MSEs
- Provided leadership training to 135 youth
- Organized ex-addict sex-workers in groups and provided them with revolving fund
- Conducted awareness meetings, produced awareness raising videos, and erected billboards
- Conducted five FGDs on the relationship between *Khat* consumption and mental illness, as there are differing views on this (and, in the Summer of 2015, unsuccessfully lobbied for budget support in order sponsor and encourage Haromaya University MA research on the relationship between mental disorder/illness and *Khat* consumption), and
- Organized an art competition/exhibition with drug addiction as its theme and with the participation of youth addicts.

Participants of the Religious Leaders and Community Elders FGD gave the following testimony on the effort that is underway by CSOs and CBOs:

> There are efforts underway by community organizations of *Ĭddïr* and *Afosha* to slow down the growing spread of *Khat* abuse, and this is allowing us to break the silence concerning *Khat*. Change is coming to Harar in this regard, particularly concerning those that are at the edge of getting into the habit and also some of those that are already in it.

3.3.3 Challenges faced and threats anticipated in realizing measures

Contrary to the widely held belief that *Khat* addicts and heavy users would have no problem to kick off the habit any time they wished to do so, the entire range of informants involved in this study, save a few, clearly and strongly affirmed the extreme difficulty involved in quitting *Khat* for good. The list below summarizes the challenges in and threats to reversing the *Khat* trend and creating conducive atmosphere for addicts and heavy users to kick off their habit. The challenges and threats, in no order of primacy, are:

- Deeply entrenched *Khat* tradition and peer pressure
- Cheap and easy availability of *Khat*
- Status of the city as being a major conduit for *Khat* export trade
- Rampant unemployment, particularly among certain groups of the city's residents
- Lack of appropriate alternative places for leisure-time activities, since all open spaces in the city have been grabbed by different interest groups
- Short duration and unsustainable funding of counter-measures, including the current CSO-CBO initiative/program
- Lack of government policy and regulation on *Khat*

Ato Wuhib Mohammad of HIAC stresses one particular challenge and a threat that is associated to it, namely the lack of financial resource sufficient enough to wage a winning fight against *Khat* and the impending danger of the discontinuation of the little that was then available, in saying:

> The fight against the spread of *Khat* consumption in Harar is not an easy task. It ought to be noted that the income of a single *Khat* trader is more than the amount of money that is provided to our organization by CSSP through the current program. Furthermore, this project's period is only 14 months, and five months have already elapsed by now. Hence, unless something is done by way of arranging for continued financing, the current activities are likely to grind to a stop.

An additional factor that absolutely deserves to be mentioned as a challenge is the sheer power of *Khat* in resisting treatment and rehabilitation of individuals who are already within its mighty clutches. This goes to the extent of patients abusing the medications they are given to make them further serve the purpose of their addiction.

What Ato Habtamu Tadesse and Wz. Aster Mulugeta, staff of the Department of Psychiatry of Hiwot Fana Specialized University Hospital jointly expressed:

> Whatever treatment we give to our patents, it is impeded by their chewing of *Khat* while under treatment. The patients that come to us are psychotic, in depression, bipolar and schizophrenic, or having one or two of these. Since most of them are psychotic, they use the sedative medication we give them for *Č'äbsi* (to break their *Khat* high).

Finally, as farmers of the surrounding area rip significantly high cash income by growing *Khat*, it will be difficult to dissuade them from doing so and supplying the growing number of consumers with affordable who grow *Khat*. Hence, unless some kind of viable crop substitution arrangement is found and implemented, it will be impossible to act on the supply side in a significant manner.

3.4 Tearing down the curtain of silence in Harar: Emerging Voices regarding *Khat*

This Subsection presents the stories of ex-*Khat* addicts and addicts in rehab in order to provide a close look at the depth of addiction the subjects of the stories had at one time sunk into and indicate the contributions of the causal and contextual factors that have helped them in escaping from the shackles of addiction in Harar. The voices of individuals who are most involved with, and affected by, *Khat* are equally, if not more, revealing of lived experiences with this captivating substance.

3.4.1 The case of Y.W, 26 year-old ex-instructor of drafting at Harar TVET and a *Khat* addict who is in rehabilitation

Y.W started chewing *Khat* at a very young age (as young as 8 years old) in the house with the knowledge of his parents. When he reached Grade Nine, his parents started giving him regular pocket money for *Khat*, in the belief that would help him study harder.

He was later employed as a teacher in a TVET College, but showed little improvement in his lifestyle because of his addiction to *Khat*. He argued that, "*Khat* makes you accept your situation and pass your days (ጫት ካለህበት ሁኔታ ጋር ተስማምተህ እንድትኖር ያደርግሀል). I did so in spite of the fact that chewing *Khat* has had several harmful impacts on me, including weight loss, insomnia, moodiness, forgetfulness, and the like. But now, having realized this, I have already reduced my consumption of *Khat* and totally stopped smoking *Shisha*."

He is in the process of being rehabilitated through the awareness creation campaigns and participation in a work groups organized with the support of SID-E. He said he now follows the maxim: 'Better to eat and weigh oneself, than to lament after chewing!' (ቅም ከማዘን፣ በልቶ መመዘን), and serves as chairman of a youth group that has seven members. He hopes to achieve good results in terms of stopping chewing *Khat* and engaging in the income generation activities of the group.

Previously, it was common for people in Harar to talk positively of *Khat* and praise it. But nowadays, due to the seriousness and widespread state of the problem there is a visible attitudinal change. People in Harar have just started to recognize the harms of *Khat*, as it has come knocking at the door of every one with some family members going totally mad, They can no longer shy away from the truth, as there are now many youngsters who have graduated from school but are still dependant on their parents; and the nuts in the city are proliferating (ጆዝባ በዛ).

3.4.2   The case of T. L, a 47 year-old ex-addict who quit *Khat* on his own

Khat is very cheap in Harar, and chewing it is socially accepted. All are for chewing *Khat*, men as well as women. In my neighborhood, people chew *Khat* as much as they want, and whenever and wherever they wish to do so. There is no limit placed on its consumption. Thus the situation in the city favors and encourages the chewing of *Khat* and hampers attempts at quitting it.

I started chewing *Khat* in 1980, continuing to do so even when I played football for a club. Gradually, I got into the habit of chewing larger amounts of *Khat* more regularly. Money was no object, as I had several well-paying jobs, first with Ethiopian Road Authority as an assistant surveyor, then with Save the Children Oromia, and with such other civil society organizations. I bought and chewed *Khat* three times a day. I also drunk cheap alcoholic drinks and smoked tobacco a lot. I would not get up and go to work once I started to chew *Khat*.

In my case, *Khat* used to arouse me to seek sex. But whenever I got to the act, the whole thing would collapse. This is generally true of most chewers. The adage "The men and the hyenas of Harar are not after people," (የሐረር ወንዶችና የሐረር ጅብ ሰው አይነካም) says it all.

I came to quit *Khat* on my own almost two months ago. I decided to stop chewing *Khat* when I was temporarily unemployed. I started getting ashamed of asking money from others to finance my *Khat* habit. I was also fed up of arguing and quarreling with

Plate 5: *Khat* market in Harar

Plate 6: A roadside *bärč'a* in progress in Harar

Plate 7: Ato young man, who has lost his teeth, preparing *khat* mash with his mortar (*Muqecha*) in Harar

Plate 8: A *Khat* captured person (Hambis) in the street of Harar

family members and others for no reason. The other reasons that encouraged me to stop chewing *Khat* were, firstly, the amount of money that I spent on *Khat* and its attendants became too much and I had to depend on others to cover my *Khat* expenses. I had sunk to the level of pawning my belongings such as my mobile to get money for the purchase of *Khat*, and I realized that quitting *Khat* would allow me to stop drinking alcohol and smoking.

Yet, It was difficult for me to quit because of the carving as well as people's comments that it was all pretention. I would be pushed into re-starting it because of the withdrawal sickness. But, the fact that my friends wouldn't believe that I have really given up *Khat* provided me with extra resolve to beat the habit. Also, going to church twice a day and prayer gave me strength. Now I have good appetite. I eat well and can manage heavy workload, and this has made me want to continue quitting *Khat*. I am certain that I will never go back to it.

There are many people that I know who have dropped out of school or quit working. They spend their whole time chewing *Khat*, getting over suspicious of other people and gradually losing their minds. There is no one in our neighborhood or community that encourage others to quit *Khat*. But, something has to be done about *Khat* in Harar since it is destroying the young generation and the society. I would also be willing to participate in any effort to help bring out others from the depth of *Khat* addiction.

3.4.3 The case of S. W, a 29 year-old ex-addict who kicked off the habit on his own

I totally quit *Khat* through my own effort in 2009 (2002 EC) after chewing *Khat* continuously for five years. I used to chew *Khat* for whole days and the nights, and I was suffering so much that I came to realize that I had to stop chewing *Khat* together with cigarette smoking.

I believed it was God's intervention that helped me to quit. One day, I heard a church father preaching against *Khat* and I felt as if he was talking to me about my situation, and advising me to quit.

When I decided to quit I also stopped all other attendant habits. I even cut my long hair and changed my appearance all together. I would stay at home keeping away from my old friends, regularly visiting the church instead.

Only a few times, did I go back to chewing a small quantity of *Khat*. But since I didn't like the feeling it created in me during these occasions, I came to hate it altogether, and realized that I had to totally avoid *Khat*. It is my relationship with God and the Church of Kidane-mehret, which I serve during Sundays, that has helped me to quit and keep off *Khat*.

While I was an addict, my addition took all of my time and took over all of my feelings. I used to work and earned enough money to cover my expenses that were all related to *Khat* and cigarettes. I didn't care much about my clothing and I rarely bought new clothes I had no realistic plans or vision for my future. I had a girlfriend, but I didn't care much about her. Finally, she left me, but that didn't affect me, as I held tight to *Khat* to be my wife.

I had a friend whose addiction had no breaks the same way as mine (እንደኔው ፍሬን የሌለው ሱስ የያዘው ነበረ). After I quit *Khat*, I began to tell him that he has to do the same, choosing the road leading to the water spring over the one into fire. But he decided to continue. On the other contrary, another elderly friend of mine followed my relentless advice and managed to quit. A third acquaintance, too, completely turn around his miserable life by overcoming his addiction to *Khat*.

As for suffering from withdrawal symptoms upon quitting *Khat*, many addicts experience strange things. One addict acquaintance of mine used to repeatedly experience *Dukak* with terrifying hallucinations that drove him to wake up in the middle of nights and scratch the walls of his bedroom with his bare fingernails until they bled.

Finally, it is true that *Khat* has an effect on the body: hazardous impacts on both the physical and mental wellbeing as well as the sexual capacity of users. There are two young people that I am well acquainted with that have gone mad after they graduated from the university.

3.4.4 The case of Ato H. T, a 26 years-old barber and would-be painter who is still a heavy *Khat* addict

Emaciated, boasting untidy and untrimmed hair and fingernails, the young man was obviously in a bad physical and mental state.

He started chewing *Khat* at the age of twelve when he was living with his aunt and working in her bar. He started chewing when other workers at the bar started to give him a small amount of *Khat* to try. He now chews *Khat* regularly, and spends about 10 Birr a day on it. Whenever he is too short of money to buy it, he shares *Khat* with his addict friends. Thus, he has no problem accessing *Khat* – at least some.

His addiction has affected his education. When he was in high school he used to take powdered *Khat* to school, as he was unable to sit in class unless he keeps on consuming *Khat*. He finally dropped out of school as *Khat* addiction took over him completely to the extent he could not keep up his attendance and abide by the rest of the school regulations.

He says that he now believes *Khat* is harmful to those who chew excessive amounts, because it leads to waste of time and money, and also causes insomnia.

He has attempted to quit chewing *Khat* in the past, but has repeatedly gone back to it, which he claims is because his lack of work to do and the resultant boredom. He wishes to stop even now and says that he will have no difficulty in quitting.

3.4.5 Cases of three ex-addicts who quit *Khat* through their own efforts, but given skills training by HIAC in order to help them to keep off

Ato AY started chewing *Khat* at a young age, although he doesn't remember the exact time. He continued to chew *Khat* when he was working in an abattoir to help him stay awake at night in the workplace. He admits that he was addicted to *Khat*, and that he was "its major victim". He got separated from his wife after they had a child together, because he wouldn't stop chewing *Khat* and she was against this. He said they got divorced because they disagreed on almost everything, and not because of impotence. Yet, he maintained that, "*Khat* leads to divorce by bringing about impotence on men;" and that he himself "used to care only for *Khat*, and did not give a damn about the 'women thing'." (ጫት ስንፈተ ወሲብ በወንድ ላይ በማስከተል ለፍች ይዳርጋል፡፡ እኔ ጫትን እንጅ የሴቱን ነገር ጉዳዬም አልለውም ነበር፡፡ ምን እንደሆነም አላውቅም ነበር፡፡)

He has stopped chewing *Khat* for the last four months, and has received training in security service. Yet, he believes that, "quitting *Khat* is a tall order. It is an addiction hard to get rid of; and *Khat* is a pimp to all other habits (ደግሞ ጫት ለሁሉም ነገር አቃጣሪ ነው). Presently, he said, his life has changed for the good because he stopped chewing *Khat*; and as he has reduced his expenditure, he is at peace with his family and healthier.

Ato S.A. got into the *Khat* habit when he, at the age of nine, left home to live on the streets. He has been chewing *Khat* in earnest since 1991. He estimates the number of days he didn't chew *Khat* since then to be not more than 30. He even engaged in theft to get money for the purchase of *Khat*. He has been in prison for theft. He reports that he even left his job because of addiction to *Khat*. He has been given training on gypsum work and now hopes to engage in work and quite chewing *Khat*. He considers himself to have been highly addicted to *Khat*, and gives the contextual factor that led him to it as follows: "In Harar, not to chew *Khat* mean to exclude oneself from social life. It is unthinkable to go empty handed, without *Khat*, even when one goes to a house of mourning".

Wz. H.T felt socially isolated when she got married and moved from her hometown of Dire Dawa to Harar in 2000; and more so after her two children started going to kindergarten rendering her awfully idle. The loneliness was intolerable, although blessed with a happy marriage and comfortable life. So, she started to regularly chew *Khat*, as it was the only way to make friends with her new female neighbors, and pass her otherwise empty leisure time. As she became addicted to *Khat*, she went beyond borrowing money from her *Bärč'a* group and started taking *Khat* on credit from the female trader. She would return home from wherever she was chewing *Khat* right before her husband who did not chew *Khat* came home. Still, friction began to emerge in her marriage, as she refused to listen to her husband and give up her newly acquired habit. She said, she bluntly told him that she couldn't quit *Khat*, even if this were to mean the end of their marriage. Now, she says she is very happy as she has stopped chewing *Khat*, is engaged in community policing work, and is leading a normal family life.

4   National-level Policy Response to Curb the Spread of *Khat* Consumption and Rehabilitate *Khat* Addicts

This work has hopefully made clear the enormity and manifoldness of the social and economic havoc wreaked by *Khat* on Ethiopian society, by building its case on the empirical investigation of the experiences of the Cities of Harar and Assosa. Furthermore, the study has shown the extent to which *Khat* has shaken the collective conscious of Ethiopian society to the extent that individuals and communities are now opening up to sound their alarm regarding the current state of things with *Khat* —a contention that is supported by other studies as well (see, for example, Cochrane and O'Regan, 2016: 6-7). The ranks of those willing to listen to the call for action appear to be on the rise. The study has also shown how community-based organized efforts to reverse the escalating spread of *Khat* have emerged, are set up and operate, and what achievements they have so far registered in Assosa and Harar. It has also revealed how these efforts, in spite of their trailblazing accomplishments, are limited in their scope and spread being at their infancy. It has found that these experimental efforts suffer from serious drawbacks on account of their lack of a national policy to be hinged on, making them dependent on external funding and giving them a makeshift appearance. Thus, the continuation of their ventures as well as their very existence is placed in doubt.

It is in consideration of all of these conclusions that have been substantiated by the findings of the empirical study that we venture to recommend and argue for a national-level policy response and countrywide measures as being imperative in order to curb the galloping spread of *Khat* consumption and addiction as well as to rehabilitate those that are already addicted to it in a humane way.

To this end, and in order to make my position on the fundamental question of the kind of policy response that is being proposed as clear as possible from the outset, I will begin by identifying the three major alternative options that are available to policy formulation —at least in theory. These are (a) to *ban the production, sale and consumption of Khat altogether* (b) to *control and restrict them through regulatory measures*, and (c) to *let the current totally permissive state of affairs continue as they are*. Cognizant of the kind of measures that are viable and acceptable under the objective conditions in Ethiopia as well as people's persistent call and support for a meaningful policy response to reverse the current trends of *Khat* consumption and addiction, it is imperative that the Federal Government of Ethiopia has to formulate a policy of legislative regulation to control and restrict the production, marketing and consumption of *Khat*, with the proviso that any of the National Regional States, their constituent Zones and *Wäräda*, as well as definite communities and institutions can promulgate and apply their own internal rules that can extend up to and including the banning of *Khat* within their respective jurisdictions —obviously within the framework of the federal government's policy.

In the subsection that follows, the wisdom of the choice of controlling and restricting *Khat* through regulation is presented as it pertains to the two main concerns in formulating policy on *Khat*, namely, economic necessity and respect for human rights. Then, the final subsection of the chapter sets forth the detailed outlines of the study's recommendation for policy formulation.

4.1 Two Main Concerns in Formulating Policy on *Khat*: Diktats of Economic Necessity and Respect for Human Rights

There is very little that is uncontroversial when it comes to *Khat*. There are arguments made from both sides of the aisle on almost all of its aspects, be they concerning its addictiveness, or impacts on the environment, economy, social life, peace and security, public health, etc. While most of the arguments that are forwarded in favor of *Khat* concerning most of these issues are often outlandish and sheer excuses, two concerns that are raised in defense of the status quo governing the production and consumption of *Khat*, namely, economic pragmatism and human rights protection, are pertinent enough from the perspective of policy making, to deserve special treatment however brief.

4.1.1 Economic considerations

Warning signals are raised on many occasions against government interference in the production and marketing of *Khat* on grounds of economic pragmatism, as those that transpired in the course of the FSS Youth and Development Dialogue Workshop dedicated to the Youth and *Khat* held on February 15, 2015 and the National Conference on *Khat* held on 12 & 13 April 2016 organized by FSS. Some participants of such events often paint a bleak picture of how measures directed at discouraging *Khat* production would ruin the millions of farmers that depend on it for their livelihood. Others even anticipate chaos and social upheaval of dire consequences to follow on the footsteps of such deterrent measures, as they would drive many economically ruined farmers into the waiting arms of illicit traders and armed rebels. Such scare mongering that are sometimes thrown as hypothetical possibilities at meetings and conferences as well as in some academic papers could have had some justification had they been specifically targeted at proposals made in favor of the total banning of the production and consumption of *Khat*[13]. But, such a draconian measure is not the only policy option that is available or that is being proposed by many sources including this study. Hence, arguments made against an extreme measure such as banning, which is not tabled by all who are concerned with the issue of policy intervention on *Khat*, cannot be used as a valid justification for abstaining from taking any action and letting *Khat* to rage unabated the way it is doing now.

A related argument that is made against regulatory intervention on the production and marketing of *Khat* holds that such a step would deprive the country of its much valued foreign exchange that it currently receives from the export of the commodity, which, at the tune of close to 300 million USD, is second only to the nation's income from coffee export. However, this argument, too, is not tenable either, on two grounds. Firstly, other things being equal, and moral considerations aside, bringing down the local consumption of *Khat*, which, according to Cochrane and O'Regan (2016: 4) accounts for the lions share of total production, through regulatory mechanisms such as the imposition of excise tax at a substantially higher rate from the current five Birr per kilogram[14], could in fact only contribute towards increasing the volume that would be available for export —the same way coffee export is being encouraged currently. Secondly, the future does not at all bode well for the continued export of *Khat* since an increasing number of its destination countries are banning its importation. Thus, working in good time and in good order towards a gradual reduction and the ultimate freeing of the County from dependence on a globally unsustainable export commodity through regulatory

---

[13]See Gebissa, 2008, for a detailed presentation of the discourse on this issue.

[14] The excise tax proclamation approved by the House of People's Representatives on July 17, 2012, declares that, "Chat locally produced and to be supplied for sale or destined for sale shall be charged at a tax rate of Birr 5 (Five Birr) per kilogram" (Proclamation No. 767/2012, Article 4).

mechanisms would be the right strategic choice even on pragmatic economic grounds alone.

An additional concern is voiced regarding the potential for instability and violence that can be precipitated by the rise of illicit market for *Khat* in the wake of strict regulation (Cochrane and O'Regan: 6). While this is a valid reason for worry, it can be raised only as regards the banning of the substance and not against regulatory or restrictive measures, as the latter do not lead to the rise of illicit markets. Lessons from the last century regarding the outcome of draconian measures against substance abuse, including that of alcoholic drinks and cannabis, leave no room for doubt concerning the mismatch between good intentions and unintended negative consequences. In the United States, the attempt to ban the consumption of alcohol during the so-called Prohibition Era failed dismally and was ultimately abandoned, but only after leaving in its wake a litter of death and destruction through the rise of illegal bootlegging, gangster-ism, and widespread corruption that came to distort its entire legal system. The experience of the Nordic countries with similar anti-alcohol measures was not any different. Even today, the same Western countries are facing similar problem on account of their problematic ban on cannabis, from which they are trying to wriggle themselves free.

Thus, the impracticality and harmfulness of attempt at totally banning the production and consumption of *Khat* are so logically obvious and historically proven, for it to be entertained as a reasonable alternative action. Such a futile exercise would only render *Khat* illegal, leading to its illicit trafficking in the hands of criminal and terrorist organizations that can flourish in the guise of "liberators."[15] Therefore, the only viable solution to the serious problem that has

---

[15] What Cochrane and O'Regan say on the current situation in Somalia and Ethiopia concerning the linkage between illicit *Khat* trade and terror groups -- or the lack of it -- is important enough to deserve being quoted at some length:

> Despite these new laws and seizures of khat, linkages between the khat trade and regional or transnational organized crime or violent groups appear ambiguous or negligible, ...there remain several degrees of separation between the two activities. In fact, khat may serve as a pull factor that mitigates piracy since "it provides one of the few industries where comparable incomes can be derived" (UNODC, 2013: 43). Additionally, in Ethiopia some khat traders operate illegally to evade export and other taxes, though they do not function as organized criminal enterprises that

invaded the fabric of Ethiopian society lies midway between the unrealistic attempt at altogether banning *Khat* on the one hand, and that of maintaining the untenable status quo, on the other; by formulating appropriate policy and passing laws that can regulate and restrict its production, marketing and consumption.

4.1.2   Human rights considerations

Arguments in defense of *Khat* on grounds of respect for human rights are heard quite often from those with vested interest in it as traders and consumers. In this regard, the recent criminalization of *Khat* as a Class-C Drug in the United Kingdom, led to a dispute that has revealed the extent to which different interest groups engage in a tug-of-war as well as the varied arguments they raise. Some saw it as the UK Government's contravention of its obligations under the International Covenant on Economic, Social and Cultural Rights (ICESCR) and other human rights instruments, since, they claim, it has ruined the livelihoods of Kenyan farmers who grow *Khat*.

Likewise, a British citizen of Somali origin, Mahamud Ahmed Mohammed, who used to engage in bulk import of *Khat* from Kenya to the United Kingdom, tried to hitch his case to individual and indigenous people cultural rights. Accordingly, he went beyond protestation to suing the then Home Secretary and current Prime minister, Theresa May, claiming that the ban on *Khat* has

---

rely on corruption or intimidation to sustain their business. Beyond this, linkages to organized crime in the country appear to be minimal.

Despite some allegations and evidence from arrests in the United Kingdom and the United States that Al Shabaab raises funds through the khat trade, the Somali Islamist militant group prohibits the sale and consumption of khat in those areas under its control. While al Shabaab has financed itself through the illegal charcoal trade, kidnapping for ransom, and taxing piracy groups, the khat ban appears to be consistently enforced. ... Al Shabaab may benefit indirectly by taxing those in the khat trade, but the overall evidence suggests that the group's involvement has been minimal.

Other than these relatively indirect connections, the khat trade in Ethiopia and the wider Horn of Africa features negligible levels of violence and weak links to violent groups or organized crime. From a purely logical standpoint, there is little reason for Ethiopian khat traders to work with organized criminal groups (Cochrane and O'Regan, 2016: 5).

infringed on his human rights. He further claimed that the use of *Khat* is part of a long-standing and established social, cultural and ethnic custom and tradition. Even more interesting enough, the court case was reportedly funded by the Kenyan government in the person of the Vice-President, William Ruto, since *Khat* farmers in Kenya would incur substantial loss of income (Independent, October 2013).

However, according to the Islamic website 5Pillars, there are many others among members of the African community in UK that hold the opposite conviction. For instance, another Somali, a social activist and anti-*Khat* campaigner by the name of Abukar Awale, has expressed his gratefulness for the UK Government's ban on *Khat* with the belief that "the vast majority of the Somali community support the ban for obvious reasons and have been cautiously optimistic that it will take effect sooner rather than later" (5Pillars, 2013: 1).

The differences in views that are indicated in the above paragraph are understandable, as they are expressions of conflicting interests. The most important issue that can be raised in connection to Human Rights and *Khat* is, therefore, the question "whose human rights" one is concerned with. There are several categories of persons that are affected differently by the production, marketing and consumption of *Khat*. Chief among these are: *Khat* farmers and their family members; operators of *Khat* processing establishments and their employees; wholesale and retail traders, owners of *Khat* dens, and more importantly its users/abusers and their family members, and if they are public servants, then the public they are meant to serve.

Interestingly enough, many organizations dedicated to fighting for respect of human rights, such as Human Rights Watch, have shown themselves to be less interested in calling for the respect of people free access and enjoyment of *Khat*, and more for the protection of the human rights and humane treatment of persons that are *Khat* users, including those that suffer from mental ailments on that account (Human Rights Watch, 2015).

The main concern of human rights advocates as regards rehabilitation and treatment of sufferers of severe *Khat* addiction and mental illness is the forced and inhuman treatment of persons committed into mental institutions. Human

Rights Watch, after revealing its findings on the linkage between mental health and *Khat* chewing in Somaliland[16], highlighted the ill-treatment of addicts and recommended, among others, that all persons with mental disabilities – including those who are *Khat* dependent – held against their will in mental health institution should be released and the practice terminated henceforth (Human Rights Watch, 2015).

On the other hand, it is also true that others have raised their voice in support of the right of individuals to use drugs. In one extreme case, a British All-Party Parliamentary Group for Drug Policy Reform has argued that the taking of drugs is a human right and that "drug laws needed to "reflect the supremacy of human rights conventions" and suggests that as long as drug taking does not harm others, it should not be a criminal offence." But, this has remained a small minority view with no real consequences; since soon after, a UK Government spokesman said that it had "no intention of decriminalizing or legalizing drugs". Furthermore, ever since the publication of this call for liberalizing the drug policy in the UK, the country has proceeded to ban *Khat*. Thus, while the trend in the Western World is generally in the direction of liberalizing the draconian laws against the circulation and use of such "entertainment drugs" as cannabis, it appears to be going in the opposite direction when it comes to the hitherto tolerated ones such as *Khat*.

Under a section of his book titled *Re-evaluation of Legal and Policy Response to Drug Use*, Norbert Gilmore proposes as follows concerning a viable reform of drug laws for the United States, that pay due attention to human rights of users:

> Any good non-prohibitionist policy has to contain three central ingredients. First, possession of small amounts of any drug for personal use has to be legal. Second, there have to be legal means by which adults can obtain drugs of certified quality, purity and quantity. These can vary from state to state and city to city, with the Federal Drug Administration playing a supervisory role in controlling quality, providing information and assuring truth in

---

[16] Many family members interviewed by Human Rights Watch in Somaliland linked their relatives' mental health problems with unemployment and what they considered to be *Khat* dependence (Human Rights Watch, 2015.

advertising. And third, citizens have to be empowered in their decisions about drugs.

A drug policy with these ingredients would decimate the black market for drugs and take out of the hands of drug lords the $50 billion to $60 billion in profits they earn each year. The nation [USA] would gain billions of dollars in law-enforcement savings and tax revenues, which could then be used to treat America's most serious problem: the miserable life prospects of millions of poor, undereducated Americans growing up in decaying, crime-ridden inner cities.

Proposals such as this should not be viewed as a rejection of prohibition (which, undoubtedly, they are), but rather as an opening gambit with which to explore ways to more effectively control drug use and prevent or minimize its harms, while ensuring respect for the human rights of everyone. (Gilmore, 2010: 23).

In sum, the current global reality, calls for the respect of human rights, including those of drug addicts. And, respect of human rights should not be seen as something that hinder the introduction of regulatory measures, but rather as a body of principles that are encapsulated in and promoted by the forgoing proposal for regulating the production, circulation and consumption of *Khat* in this country. Hence, human rights should be considered and advocated both as the means and the end of a concerted effort to deal with the needs of *Khat* victims and all aspects of the dramatically swelling problem —if, unfortunately, not to altogether do away with it.

There is a second aspect of human rights that is already referred to in the preceding page, but that needs further elaboration. This has to do with protection of the right of a social, ethnic or cultural group to enjoy freely its long-standing tangible and non-tangible customary and traditional assets. Without doubt, the culturally regulated use of *Khat* in some parts of the Horn of Africa and Southern Arabia was such a traditional practice, and hence could be considered as something covered by the principle of human rights as referred to by the Universal Declaration of Human Rights.

However, it is quite difficult to appeal to this right under present day conditions, because the practice of *Khat* use has shaded off its original socially domesticated character becoming something else in those places and among those groups to which it has migrated. Its nature has in fact not remained the same even in its place of origin, having been under the influence of outside forces and incoming people of other cultural orientations. Thus, in a world steamrolled by globalization, there is little room left for national exceptionalism, let alone local ones. Hence, protecting the production, circulation and consumption of *Khat* in the name of respecting long-standing traditional practices is impractical. What is viable in the case of Ethiopia is to deal with the escalating spread of the *Khat* phenomenon, the adverse impacts of which by far outweigh its questionable economic advantage to the society, through realistic and fair policy and legal responses that take the interest of all that are involved in the business as producers, traders and consumers into consideration.

4.2   Recommendation on National Policy Direction

4.2.1   Actors' recommendations from Assosa

This Subsection presents recommendations garnered during the fieldwork informing the study from all categories of actors involved in one way or another with *Khat*: government officials, CSO and CBO leaders, community representatives, addicts, ex-addicts, and addicts in rehabilitation in Assosa. The following list summarizes the major recommendations that have been garnered in the course of the fieldwork, without any order of primacy:

- Comprehensive law which regulates all aspects of *Khat* such as converting one's farm to *Khat* production, taxation, location of *Khat* selling places, who and where one can buy, chew it, etc.

- Work done by CSOs is exemplary, but of low scale. Thus the government has to involve and expand the work being done on mitigating the adverse impacts of *Khat* addiction.

- Further in-depth study that looks into the various aspects of *Khat* consumption such as the rural-urban linkage, etc.

- Include *Khat* related subjects in Civic and Ethical Education Courses and their textbooks

- Universities have to have strict rules / implement the rules they have regarding chewing *Khat*, and

- Help *Khat* growers to adopt high value/high yield crops so that they can replace their *Khat* crop without much financial loss.

4.2.2 Actors' recommendations from Harar

This Subsection presents recommendations garnered during the fieldwork informing the study from all categories of actors involved in one way or another with *Khat*: Government officials, CSO and CBO leaders, community representatives, addicts, ex-addicts, and addicts in rehabilitation in Harar.

When it comes to the recommendation of informants concerning which way to go and what concrete measures to take given the current situation of the *Khat* epidemic, a couple of generalization can be made. Firstly, there were no informants, whatever their way of life and whatever their addiction status, who proposed a laisser-faire solution by which the current state of affairs should be allowed to continue unhampered. Secondly, all informants called for the introduction of government intervention through appropriate policy, regulation and control, to one extent or another and in one form or another. Although their recommendations were varied in form, it is possible to summarize them as follows since they are similar in substance and spirit:

The solution in restricting the spread of *Khat* should not consist of immediately jumping into imposing regulatory measures. It ought to be preceded with the formulation of well thought-out policy that is informed by research, and then by taking steps such as the following:

- Create awareness of the adverse impacts of *Khat* on the individual and the community
- Provide the farmers with viable substitute crops such as apples
- Look for alternative income generation activities for those engaged in *Khat* trade
- Impose high tariff on *Khat*, in order to make it less affordable
- Make *Khat* sale and purchase as orderly and as difficult as possible by imposing strict marketing rules
- Get children out of the *Khat* trade and away from *Khat* related services

- Focus on peer-group pressure as well as cultural and social enablers of *Khat*, in order to turn them around
- Work with religious groups and institutions (both Christian and Moslem) that discourage the consumption of *Khat* by their members as well as by others that they get in touch with
- Provide for appropriate alternative places of outdoor and indoor leisure-time activities, and
- Provide for appropriate treatment and rehabilitation of individuals that are heavily addicted to *Khat* and physically and mentally sick.

4.2.3   Suggestions for a National Policy Response

The discussion hereunder is based on the above policy recommendations of the actor-informants in Assosa and Harar, the indications garnered from the discussion conducted during the two-day National Conference in general and its concluding panel discussion on policy and intervention in particular[17], as well as desk reviews of existing policy and legal instruments of the Government of Ethiopia and comments regarding the same obtained from government officials at the federal level. It thus represents a synthesis of policy related inputs obtained from these four sources.

The total absence of a policy framework is attested by a quick look at the *National Social Policy* (2014), the *GTP II Document* (2014) and the *Proclamation to Provide for Food, Medicine and Health Care Administration and Control* (2010). None of this documents that raise all sorts of social problems faced by the country and attempt to provide solutions to them, do not even mention the term *Khat*, let alone to proceed to acknowledge it as a source of problems and indicate the way out.

---

[17] The draft report of this study, together with several others papers, was presented and discussed at a two-day National Conference held on 12 & 13 April 2016 and attended by stakeholders and experts. Together with, informal interviews conducted with and brief communications obtained from national-level stakeholders and players: Well-known psychiatrists engaged in the treatment of drug induced mental illness, as well as officials of the Dangerous Drugs Division of the Federal Police Commission and those of FMHACA and MoLSA. The National Conference, in which these experts and officials made presentations and/or constituted the panel that led its closing discussion on policy, has indicated the general direction and pathways that the future formulation of national-level policy and intervention nee to follow in order to deal with the *Khat* conundrum in the country.

Surprisingly enough, the last mentioned instrument, the proclamation that provided for FMHACA, which is closest to the issue, chose to remain mute concerning *Khat* after having declared in no uncertain terms about all edibles, that includes it, as follows:

> "Food" means any raw, semi-processed or processed substance for commercial purpose or to be served for the public in any way intended for human consumption that includes water and other drinks, chewing gum, supplementary food and any substance which has been used in the manufacture, preparation or treatment of food, but does not include tobacco and substances used only as medicines (Proclamation No. 661/2009. 2010: Article 2, Sub-article 1).

Thus, even this proclamation that came close to providing for the regulation of the circulation and use of *Khat*, forfeited an opportunity to deal with a major societal menace. Furthermore, even the five-page agreement document duly signed and stamped in November 2012 between the Federal Ministry of Labor and Social Affairs (MoLSA) and the Ethiopian Food, Medicine and Health Care Administration and Control Authority (FMHACA) to *Work in Unison and Coordination in order to Control and Reduce the Circulation and Use of Dangerous Illicit Drugs and Plants*, does not list the drugs and plants that it targets, let alone mentioning *Khat* by name. The provisions for control that are enumerated in the document, also reveal the fact that the intention of the agreement falls too short of addressing the glaring policy and legal shortfalls and instead pays heed to educational and awareness raising activities.

Due to the above shown glaring lacuna in policy and regulation, as well as on the basis of what has been learnt through the fieldwork informing this study, from the discussions conducted in the course of the two-day National Conference held on 12 & 13 April 2016, it is safe to conclude that the major pitfall in dealing with the *Khat* problem that has overwhelmed the country is the lack of a coherent national policy providing for appropriate strategies and regulations. Only a small number of discussants at the above-mentioned National Conference were found to espouse the opposite view, often with the worn-out argument that the *Khat* question is too contentious to deal with.

Quite surprisingly, a 45-page 2011 government document reporting the findings of a study on Exogenous Cultural and Traditional Practices and their Negative Impacts on the Residents of Addis Ababa, particularly the Youth and Women, by the City Government of Addis Ababa Women, Children & Youth Affairs Bureau, candidly admits not only the vicious grasp that *Khat* has on the people of Addis Ababa in general and the youth in particular, but laments the absence of policy and legal framework to deal with it. In fact, the document goes to the extent of spelling out the contradictions in the legal provisions governing *Khat* and Shisha, and the impossible task of authorities engaged in controlling Shisha and *Khat* dens in very vivid terms[18].

Many important professional associations and civil society organizations, including the influential Ethiopian Public Health Association, too, have forcefully advocated for the regulation of the marketing and consumption of *Khat* (see Annex Two). Likewise, renowned practicing psychiatrists of the country who are engaged in treating the victims of *Khat*, among others, as well as drug control officers currently engaged in fighting the circulation of illicit

---

[18] The relevant paragraphs of the document, which deserves to be quoted in full, read as follows:

ከፍትህ ቢሮና ከፖሊስ የተገኘው መረጃ እንደሚያሳየው፣ኢትዮጵያ በዓለም አቀፍ ደረጃ ስምምነት የተደረሰበትን የተባበሩት መንግስታት ያወጣውን የአደንኛ ዕፅ ክልከላን የተመለከተ ህግ ተቀብላ በወንጀል ህግ በአንቀጽ 525 አካታለች። በድንጋጌው መሰረትም፣ ማንኛውንም መርዛማ የናርኮቲክ ወይም የሳይኮትሮፒክ መድሃኒቶችን ልዩ ፈቃድ ሳይኖረው፣ ወደ ሀገር ውስጥ በመስገባት፣ በማክፋፈል፣ በማዘዋወር፣ በማብቀል ወይም በማፍብረክ ስራ ላይ የተሳተፈ ማንኛውም ሰው፣ ህግ በመተላለፍ ወንጀል እንደሚጠየቅና በእስራትና በገንዘብ እንደሚቀጣ ቢገልጽም፣ በአሁኑ ሰዓት በአገራችን ከፍተኛ ችግር እየፈጠረ ያለና ብዙ ወጣቶችና ቤቶችን ላልተገቡ ባህሪያት ብሎም ለወንጀል እየዳረገ ያለው ሺሻና ጫት መሆኑ ተጠቁሟል። ይህ በወንጀል ህጋችን ውስጥ ግልፅ ክልከላ ያልተደረገበት ሲሆን ሌሎች ሀገሮች ግን ህግ ማውጣታቸውን መረጃ ሰጭዎች አስረድተዋል።

የጥናቱ መረጃ በተጨማሪም ከጫትና ሺሻ ጋር በተያያዘ በሀገራችን ያለው ህግ እርስ በርሱ እንደሚጣረስ አመልክቷል። ይህ አስመልክቶ መንግስት በአንድ በኩል ለሺዲዮ ቤቶች ፍቃድ ይሰጣል በሌላ በኩል ደግሞ ስለ ጎጂነቱ ያወራል፣ ይህ ተጣጣሞ መሄድ የማይችል ነገር ነው። በተጨማሪም፣ ሺሻ ቤቶች ተስፋፍተው የሚገኙበት ሁኔታ አለ። እነዚህን ሺሻ ቤቶች በተመለከተ መንግስት በየወቅቱ የማጥፋት ዘመቻ ያካሄዳል፣ ሺሻውንና ማጨሻውን አይሰበሰበ ያቃጥላል፣ ነገር ግን ይህን ስራ የሚከለክልና የሚቀጣ ህግ ስለሌለ ዕቃውን መልሰው በመግዛት ስራውን ይጀምራሉ። ሌላው ጫት ነው፣ ጫት በሀገራችን ኢኮኖሚ ትልቅ ድርሻ አለው ብለን ብንወስድም ችግሩ ግን ከአቅም በላይ እየሆነ ነው። ከዚህ ጋር ተያይዞ ህፃናትና ወጣቶች እየተበላሹ ያሉበት ሁኔታ ይስተዋላል። "የፈለግኩትን ስራ መስራትም ሆነ መጠቀም መብቴ ነው" በሚል እነዚህን አላፈላጊ ዕፆች ማስፋፋትም ሆነ መጠቀም ሀብረተሰቡ ከማይደዋጣው ችግር ውስጥ እየከተተ ስለሆነ "ለመብትም ገደብ ሊበጅለት ይገባል" በማለት መረጃ ሰጭዎቹ ገልጸዋል። (በአዲስ አበባ ከተማ አስተዳደር የሴቶች፣ ህፃናትና ወጣቶች ጉዳይ ቢሮ፣ ህዳር 2004 እ.ኢ.አ፣ ገፅ 24)።

substances, have expressed their serious concerns and the need to act without delay in order to reverse the galloping spread of *Khat* abuse. They did this in their interviews for the benefit of this study, as well as in their repetitive communications over the media and at the above-mentioned National Conference on *Khat* that was held on 12 & 13 April 2016 under the auspices of the Forum for Social Studies.

It is still noteworthy that many informants and discussants are aware and wary of the difficulty in dealing with the *Khat* problem. Hence they favor and recommend careful, comprehensive, and knowledge-based policy formulation and intervention. With all of this in mind, we can at this point proceed to present a sketchy outline of a way forward, beginning with a couple of suggestions regarding the environment and the context within which the discourse leading to a viable policy can be worked out:

- Extremist positions will not do, and must be avoided in the discourse leading to the formulation of appropriate and viable policy. A total ban on *Khat* is equally undoable as laissez-faire of letting it to continue as it is, would be destructive; and those who take the former extreme position are actually in league with those who argue in favor of the opposite, the same way politicians that call for the total banning of guns in the US play into the hands of those who don't want to hear a word about gun control.

- Search for a singular solution based on the belief of "one fits all" is counter productive, as the situation in different parts of the country and of the different sectors of the society are not exactly the same as attested by the findings of the study in Assosa and Harar.

- Considering the sensitiveness of the issue of *Khat*, discourses and narratives leading to the expected policy formulation need to be undertaken with sensitivity, empathy, and respect for the feelings of all concerned. The campaign against *Khat* ought to be waged with the objective of demonizing *Khat* abuse and not its users.

- Cognizant of the likelihood that there would be losers and winners – some in the short-run and others in the long-run – from any policy induced change of the current *Khat* scene, all effort ought to be made to find fair and just solution that address and ways to reconcile the seemingly incompatible interests of stakeholders.

- Finally, in order to preempt the likelihood of causing misconceptions and misunderstandings among the public, as is the case particularly with the planned reform of traditionally established practices, conducting genuine and transparent public discussion and debate over the mass media and community assemblies is crucial.

Without loosing sight of the above, it is possible to give an outline of the kind of regulations that brings together and addresses the diverse recommendations and suggestions that have transpired both in the findings of the fieldwork and during the two-day National Conference. And these are:

A. Formulate and implement realistic regulations to control the currently unfettered spread of *Khat* consumption and addiction; along the following outline:
  - Production: If the policy option of banning the consumption of *Khat* is rejected in favor regulating it, then it becomes absolutely necessary to:

    a. Regulate and guarantee the *Khat* that is supplied to the public is as safe as much as it is practically possible. Considering, in particular, the current practice of spraying *Khat* plants with chemicals such as *malathion* and DDT by farmers, the federal agency in charge of food and drugs administration, FMHACA, and the Ministry of Agriculture and Environmental Protection as well as the MoH and MoT, must jointly set up mechanisms by which the long-term interests of the producers and consumers of *Khat* as well as those of the society at large are guaranteed. These mechanisms can include regulating by whom and within what terms *Khat* ought to be produced, processed, and might involve systems of licensing and quality control.

    b. Undertake measures through which farmers are encouraged and supported to free themselves from dependence on the production of *Khat*. The measures in question should include, but not be limited to, a crop substitution program that is facilitated by the provision of subsidy of fixed duration.

- Transport: The manner and means under which *Khat* is transported from points of production and processing to places of consumption is of great concern to the society. It is common for all types of motor vehicles carrying fresh *Khat* to meander their way up and down dangerous routes in order to deliver their consignments as early as possible before the *Khat* loses its potency due to its famous short shelf life, on the one hand, and so as to beat competitors to the point of destination or the market site thereby fetching higher price, on the other. This common means of *Khat* transportation has become a source of many traffic accidents, death and destruction. This state of affairs has reached a point where it can no longer be tolerated, and it is therefore necessary for government to formulate appropriate policy informing a new code of conduct to be imposed on the transportation of *Khat*. The system of control in this respect must regulate the types and state of the vehicles, the terms under which they operate, as well as the competencies, special duties and conditions that are required of the drivers while on and off-duty.

- Trade: In today's Ethiopia, *Khat* is sold and bought by whomever, wherever, and whenever it pleases one. Underage children can purchase it from a stall that is located right in front of their school, place of worship or home. Its sale is driven by attractive commercials that adorn the sides of avenues, roads and public squares. This easy to *Khat*, together with the permissive facilitation of its trade, has contributed to its escalating consumption by all age groups, genders, and socioeconomic status groups. The minimum that the Ethiopian society and its government can do, is to regulate the domestic sale of *Khat*, by regulating the location and working hours of its outlets, the type of persons that can legally engage in its trade, as well as banning its advertisement in public places all together.

- Consumption: In the same manner as it is traded, *Khat* is consumed at all sites and in all manners that are regulated neither by law nor by custom. Such practice, in addition to making consumption something easy-to-do, also contributes to the permissive attitude towards *Khat* and accelerated spread of consumption that follows. It is therefore imperative to control the places of consumption as well as the category of persons that are permitted to consume *Khat*. Such a regulation can have far reaching consequences on the attraction and acceptability of *Khat* among future generations in particular.

- Cost covering/recovering: The economic as well as the social cost of *Khat* consumption are now things that are borne by society as a whole and not by those who indulge in it alone. Thus, *Khat*'s impacts remain as what economists refer to as externalities and those who chew it as free riders. All members of the society, including those that have nothing to do with *Khat* are forced to pick the bills on an equal level as those that do. Such is the case not only concerning current costs, but even more importantly future accounts. All of the country's taxpayers would be the ones to pay for all the health, crime, environmental, and infrastructural damages caused by those who enjoy the freedom of chewing *Khat* and those others who profit from the business. Therefore, excise-tax (a) that is high enough to discourage the consumption of *Khat* by raising its selling price (b) that justly allocates costs to those that are responsible in creating them in the first place, and (c) that is capable of generating sufficient income to society to deal with the costs of *Khat*, is essential. Such a system ought to aim at assigning the short and long-term costs of *Khat* consumption and addiction to those who choose to chew it, to be covered in such a way that chewers and those involved in the business pay forward the costs of their actions the same way societies all over the world employ mechanisms of cost recovery on liquor and tobacco, lest they remain as externalities.

- Awareness creation and behavioral change: Hand-in-hand with the above mentioned regulatory measures, veritable and sustainable campaigns aimed at (a) persuading the young to resist peer-pressure and remain free of *Khat* by raising their awareness of its harmful impacts, among others by including the subject in school curricula such as the Civic and Ethical Education Courses (b) working on those that are "on-and-off" users to convince them to totally abstain in good time from *Khat* chewing lest they may not be gradually drawn into its inescapable clutches, and (c) persuading and supporting those *Khat* users that are already into it, to either kick off the habit altogether or reduce their consumption level so as to minimize its effects on them. In order to achieve these aims, certain strategies need to be employed; and chief among these, are (a) exposing the impacts of *Khat* addiction in no uncertain terms through the media, in public gatherings, community conversations, etc. and (b) employing the participation of CBOs, CSOs, youth groups, and religious organizations of all denominations.

B. Formulate and implement appropriate strategies for addressing the consultation, treatment and rehabilitation needs of persons that are already addicted to *Khat*; among other, through:
  - Significantly expanding and improving the service offered by existing rehabilitation and treatment centers and institutions, as well as by establishing new ones that are up to acceptable standards

  - Mainstreaming mental health care in all hospitals and into primary care provision

- Guarantee access to mental health treatment for all on the basis of free and informed consent in order to protect the human rights and privacy of persons using such services

- Looking into the possibility of, and experimenting with ways of providing treatment and rehabilitation services to *Khat* addicts as they are within their community and without being institutionalized

- Training and recruiting highly qualified and specialized psychiatrist, psychologists, medium level generalists social workers, as well as mainstreaming mental health treatment in the training of medical doctors, and

- Integrating and replicating the lessons learnt through the experience of CSOs, CBOs and government agencies in regard to the treatment and rehabilitation of persons addicted to *Khat*, and involving such experienced agents in improved and sustainable future activities.

Finally, a few words on the reciprocal relations between *Khat* and the wider world are in order. These days, there are no societal phenomena, institutions, and even events in any individual country that are exempt from the steamroller effect of globalization. Technological developments and demographic processes have made the distribution and consumption of *Khat* a matter of concern for the world in general, and the developed countries in particular. The latter, which once looked upon *Khat* as mere curiosity that can be safely ignored as a faraway regional problem, are now forced to deal with it because the immigration of hundreds of thousands of people from the traditional homes of the substance has brought into their countries a Trojan horse that can no longer be disregarded.

Counter measures taken in some countries, too, affect related processes in other countries, and destination countries of the *Khat* trade have not passively watched the escalating import of *Khat* into their countries. In fact, many of them have reacted by taking harsh measures. From 1971 up to 2014, 24 countries have criminalized the use -- and hence the importation and distribution -- of *Khat* treating it as a controlled substance. The long and growing list of such countries includes: Rwanda, Saudi Arabia, Israel, China, Malaysia, Philippines, United Arab Emirates, United Kingdome, Ireland, France, Germany, Belgium, Sweden, Norway, Denmark, Finland, Iceland, Poland, Romania, United States, Canada, Australia, and New Zealand. Even some countries from the region such as Eritrea and Tanzania have joined the ranks of those that are fighting *Khat* by banning it, while a similar legislative process is underway in the Ugandan Parliament (Cochrane and O'Regan: 2016: 4). The seriousness with which the measures are being implemented by the countries that have banned *Khat*, is exemplified by the fact that, "seizures of *Khat* and arrests for its trade in Europe, the United States, and China have spiked in recent years. The quantity of *Khat* seized in Europe since 2001 increased nearly tenfold, with recent spikes in France and Germany" (Cochrane and O'Regan: 2016: 4).

Other countries, such as those in Latin America, have no legislation on *Khat*, apparently because they do not yet harbor significant numbers of its users and are there for destinations of its illicit trade. Not surprisingly, the use of, and trade in, *Khat* are officially or unofficially considered legal only in countries of the Horn of Africa, namely, Ethiopia, Kenya, Somalia, Djibouti, and Yemen. The other exceptions in this regard are Thailand and Indonesia, which have explicitly legalized *Khat*, for no obvious reason. The World Health Organization (WHO), the international agency mandated to regulate the use of all types of drugs, appears to be somewhat ambivalent towards the use of *Khat*. While it has classified *Khat* as a drug of abuse in 1980 on the ground that it can produce psychological dependence (Nutt, *et al*, 2007*)*, it does not consider *Khat* addiction to be seriously problematic (Al-Mugahed, 2008).

What emerges from what has been said in the above paragraphs is that the future appears to be bleak for the unregulated global trade and use of *Khat*. It seems that, with the passage of time, the geographic as well as the legal space within which the trade, distribution and use of *Khat* can precede unabated will get narrower and tighter. No country can, therefore, afford to ignore and continue to be out of step from the international community. Hence, the sooner Ethiopia finds ways with which to get out of the double bind of galloping *Khat* production and consumption, the better it will find itself in tune with the requirements of the global reality.

5 Concluding Remarks

The study, the findings of which are reported in this book, has been both extensive and intensive. It was extensive, in that it has covered the various aspects of the *Khat* phenomenon, albeit, to varying degrees. Thus, *Khat's* introduction and spread, its prevalence, patterns of consumption, its socioeconomic impacts, and measures that are underway to counter its escalation in the two cities of Assosa and Harar that are the main geographical focus of the study were all covered by the study. However, those features of *Khat* that are outside its consumption proper, such as its production, preparation for sale, marketing and value chain, are either briefly described or only mentioned in passing.

Those socioeconomic issues that relate to the consumption of and addiction to *Khat* are thoroughly covered by the study and their multifarious impacts identified, analyzed and categorized to permit systematically worked out generalizations. The in-depth nature of this study that has by and large relied on qualitative approach has permitted the perceptions of its various categories of informants pertaining to their lived experience to surface, and their voices to be heard directly. In this sense, the study has made a fresh contribution to the growing literature on the *Khat* enigma in Ethiopia.

In seeking to base the search for future policy directions on lesson drawn from counter measures that are already being taken by communities, GOs, NGOs, CBOs and CSOs, the reactions and responses of the local and wider society in the two cities as well as in the country as a whole, were given due attention and properly studied. This effort has led to the identification of the state of what have been done in this regard this far including their limitations, challenges, potentials, as well as the recommendation of the local as well as the national-level actors for the way forward in formulating a viable national policy on *Khat*.

This volume represents an already condensed form of a large amount of material collected in the form of audio, video, photo, transcript and observational notes, not to mention the secondary archival material such as data sets and published works. Hence, to try to further compress what has been presented in the preceding chapters by attempting to give "a summary of findings" at this point would have only led to the loss of the gist of the important matters already in the text, covering: (a) the various aspects of the escalating consumption of and addiction to *Khat,* including their socioeconomic impacts (b) the present state of responses that are underway, and (c) by way of recommendation, an outline to serve future policy formulation efforts. Readers would benefit more by consulting the respective chapters and sections on these issues, while those with little time to spare can always refer to the short *Policy Brief* of the study that is published both in English and Amharic by the Forum for Social Studies (FSS).

References

5Pilars. 2013. Thank you Britain for banning *Khat*.
http://5pillarsuk.com/2013/08/01/thank-you-britain-for-banning-*Khat*/

Alem, A., and Shibre, T.1997. *Khat*-induced Psychosis and its Medico-legal
Implication: A Case Report. *Ethiopian Journal of Medicine*. 35, 137–139.

Al-Mugahed, Leen. 2008. "*Khat* Chewing in Yemen: Turning over a New Leaf: *Khat*
Chewing Is on the Rise in Yemen, Raising Concerns about the Health and
Social Consequences" *Bulletin of the World Health Organization. 86 (10):
741–2*.

Banjaw, M.Y., Miczek, K., Schmitdt, W.J.. 2006. Repeated catha edulis oral
administration enhances the baseline aggressive behavior in isolated rats.
Journal of Neural Transmission. 113, 543–556.

Bassil KL, Vakil C, Sanborn M, Cole DC, Kaur JS, Kerr KJ. October 2007. Cancer
health effects of pesticides: systematic review. *Canadian Family Physician*.
53(10): 1704-11.

Benishangul-Gumuz Development Association Network (BGDAN). Undated.
Baseline Survey. Assosa.

Binyam Negussie, Melake Damena and Gudina Egata. 2014 'Substance use,
prevalence and determinant factors among high school students in Dire Dawa
Administrative Council, Eastern Ethiopia'. JIMMA-MINNESOTA
International Symposium on Mental Health and Substance Use. 17-19,
FEBRUARY 2014. Jimma University.

Burton, Richard, 1856. Full Text of *First Footsteps in East Africa: or An Exploration
of Harar*. In two volumes. Vol. I. Edited by his wife Isabel Burton. Tylston
and Edwards. London.

Cochrane, L., and D. O'Regan. 2016. Legal harvest and illegal trade: Trends,
challenges, and options in *Khat* production in Ethiopia. *International Journal
of Drug Policy*. http://dx.doi.org/10.1016/j.drugpo.2016.02.009

CSA. 2008. Summary and Statistical Report of the 2007 Population and Housing
Census, Federal Democratic Republic of Ethiopia Population Census
Commission. Central Statistical Agency, Addis Ababa.

CSA. 2012a. Ethiopia Demographic and Health Survey 2011. Central Statistical
Agency, Addis Ababa.

CSA. 2012b. Welfare Monitoring Survey 2011, Statistical Report, Indicators on
Living Standard, Accessibility and Household Assets, Vol II. Central
Statistical Agency, Addis Ababa.

Carmichael, Tim. 2000. Discussing the Leaf of Allah: Linguistic Aspects of Qat Culture in Harar, Ethiopia. *Ufahamu: A Journal of African Studies. UCLA.*

Federal Democratic Republic of Ethiopia. National Planning Commission. May 2016. Growth and Transformation Plan II (GTP II) (2015/16-2019/20). Volume I: Main Text. Addis Ababa.

Federal Democratic Republic of Ethiopia. National Social Protection Policy. November 2014 Addis Ababa

Federal Democratic Republic of Ethiopia. January 2010. Proclamation to Provide for Food, Medicine and Health Care Administration and Control. Proclamation No. 661/2009. Federal Negarit Gazeta. 16th year, No. 9. Addis Ababa.

Federal Democratic Republic of Ethiopia. August 2012. Proclamation on Chat Excise Tax. Proclamation No. 767/2012. Federal Negarit Gazeta. 18th Year, No. 60. Addis Ababa.

Gebissa, E. 2008. Scourge of life or an economic lifeline? Public discourses on *Khat* (Catha edulis) in Ethiopia. *Substance Use & Misuse*, 43, 784–802

Gete Tesgaye. 2007 EC. 'Substance use and its psychological, social, economic and health impacts'. In Zerihun Mohammed (ed.), *Youth and Development in Ethiopia*. Addis Ababa: FSS (in Amharic)

Gessesse Dessie, 2013 'Favoring a Demonized Plant: *Khat* and Ethiopian Smallholder-Enterprises', *Current African Issues*. No. 51, Uppsala: Nordiska Afrikainstitutet.

Gilmore, Norbert. 2010. Drug Use and Human Rights: Privacy, Vulnerability, Disability and Human Rights Infringements. file:///I|/drugtext/local/library/books/gilmore/impact.htm [16-8-2010 15:15:21].

Girma Negash. 2017. *The Impact of Khat on Children's Education: A Comparative Study of Two Khat Producing and Marketing Centers In Southern and Eastern Ethiopia*. Forum for Social Studies. Addis Ababa.

Human Rights Watch. 2015. Chained Like Prisoners: The abuse of people with mental health condition in Somaliland. https://www.hrw.org/report/2015/10/25/chained-prisoners/abuses-against-people-psychosocial-disabilities-somaliland.

Independent. October 2013. Kenya funds lawsuit against Theresa May's ban on herbal stimulant *Khat*: Trader claims criminalizing stimulant herb violates human rights of African users in UK. http://www.independent.co.uk/news/uk/politics/kenya-funds-lawsuit-against-theresa-may-s-ban-on-herbal-stimulant-*Khat*-8890187.html

Jurewicz, J. and Hanke W. 2008. Prenatal and childhood exposure to pesticides and neurobehavioral development: review of epidemiological studies. *International Journal of Occupational Medicine and Environmental Health.* 21(2): 121-32. doi: 10.2478/v10001-008-0014-z

Kennedy, John. G. 1987. The Flower of Paradise: The Institutionalized Use of the Drug Qat In North Yemen. D. Reidel Publishing Company. Dordrecht / Boston / Lancaster / Tokyo.

Lemieux, Andrien, Li Bingshuo and Mustafa al'Absi. 2014. *Khat* use and appetite: An overview and comparison of amphetamine, *Khat* and cathinone. 2014. *Journal of Ethnopharmacol.* Published online 2014 Nov 28. doi: 10.1016/j.jep.2014.11.002

Marshall, Norma and Jane Hendtlass. 1986. Drugs & Prostitution, *Journal of Drug Issues.* Sage Journals. Vol. 16, Issue 2.

Mwenda, J.M., M.M. Arimi, M.c. Kyama and D.k. Langat. June 2003. Effects of *Khat* (Catha Edulis) Consumption on Reproductive Functions: A Review. *East African Medical Journal.* Vol. 80 No.6.

Nutt, D., King, L.A, Saulsbury, *C.*, Blakemore, Colin. March 2007. Development of a rational scale to assess the harm of drugs of potential misuse. *Lancet. 369 (9566): 1047–53.*

Odenwald, M., Lingenfelder, B., Peschel, W., 2008. Psychotic Disorder, *Khat* Abuse and Aggressive Behavior in Somalia: A Case Report. *African Journal of Drug and Alcohol Studies.* 7, 59–63.

Pantelis, Christos, Charles G. Hindler and John C. Taylor. 1989. Use and abuse of *Khat* (Catha edulis): a review of the distribution, pharmacology, side effects and a description of psychosis attributed to *Khat* chewing. *Psychological Medicine.* 19, 657-668.

Philpart, M., Goshu, M., Gelaye, B., Williams, M.A., Berhane, Y., 2009. Prevalence and Risk Factors of Gender-based Violence Committed by Male College Students in Awassa Ethiopia. *Violence and Victims.* 24, 122c–136.

Sanborn M, Kerr KJ, Sanin LH, Cole DC, Bassil KL, Vakil C. 2007 October. Non-cancer health effects of pesticides: systematic review and implications for family doctors. *Canadian Family Physician.* 53(10): 1712-20.

Solomon Tefera. 2016. "*Khat* and Health with Emphasis on Its Impact on Mental Health". In Asnake Kefale and Zerihun Mohammed (eds.) *Multiple Faces of Khat in Ethiopia.* Addis Ababa: Forum For Social Studies (FSS)

Yadeta Dessie, Jemal Ebrahim and Tadesse Awo. 2013. Mental Distress among University Students in Ethiopia: A Cross-sectional Survey. *PanAfrican Medical Journal* (open Access).

Yeraswork Admassie and Ezana Amdework. 2010. The *Araké* Dilemma: The Socioeconomics of Traditional Distilled Alcohol Production, Marketing, and Consumption in Ethiopia. Forum for Social Studies (FSS). Addis Ababa. ISBN: 978-99944-5036-7

Yeshigeta Gelaw and Abraham Haile-Amlak. 2004. *Khat* chewing and its socio-demographic correlates among the Staff of Jimma University. *Ethiopian Journal of Health Development* 18 (3): 179-184.

የቤኒሻንጉል ጉሙዝ ልማት ማህበራት ህብረት። 2007 እ.ኢ.አ። *ከሱስ የፀዳ ትውልድ እንፍጠር*። ልሳነ-ልማት። 4ኛ ዕትም። አሶሳ። (Benishangul-Gumuz Development Organizations Coalition. 2014. *Let's create a Generation that is Khat Clean*. Lisane-Limat. No. 4. Assosa).

የቤኒሻንጉል ጉሙዝ ልማት ማህበራት ህብረት። 2008 እ.ኢ.አ። *ከሱስ የፀዳ ዜጋ ለልማት*። ልሳነ-ልማት። 5ኛ ዕትም። አሶሳ። (Benishangul-Gumuz Development Organizations Coalition. 2015. *Khat Clean Citizen for Development*. Lisane-Limat. No. 5. Assosa).

በሠራተኛና ማህበራዊ ጉዳይ ሚኒስቴር እና በኢትዮጵያ የምግብ፣ የመድኃኒትና ጤና ክብካቤ አስተዳደርና ቁጥጥር ባለሥልጣን። ህዳር 2005 እ.ኢ.አ። *የአደገኛ መድኃኒቶችና እፆች ሕገ-ወጥ ዝውውርና አጠቃቀም3 ለመከላከልና ለመቀነስ በትብብርና በቅንጅት የተፈረመ የመግባቢያ ስምምነት*። (Ministry of Labor and Social Affairs and the Food, Medicine and Health Care Administration and Control Authority. 2012. *Agreement to Work in Unison and coordination in order to Control and Reduce the Circulation and Use of Dangerous Illicit Drugs and Plants*. Addis Ababa).

በአዲስ አበባ ከተማ አስተዳደር የሴቶች፣ ህፃናትና ወጣቶች ጉዳይ ቢሮ። ህዳር 2004 እ.ኢ.አ። *መጤ ባህሎችና ልማዳዊ ድርጊቶች በአዲስ አበባ ከተማ ነዋሪዎች፣ በተለይም በወጣቶችና ሴቶች ላይ እያስከተሉ ያለው አሉታዊ ተፅዕኖ*። አዲስ አበባ። (City Government of Addis Ababa Women, Children & Youth Affairs Bureau. November 2011. *Exogenous Cultural and Traditional Practices and their Negative Impacts on the Residents of Addis Ababa, Particularly the Youth and Women*. City Government of Addis Ababa. Addis Ababa).

ወልደ አማኑኤል ጉዲሶ። ጥር 2007 እ.ኢ.አ። *ወጣቱና ጫት፣ የመቃም ታሪክ ከአዝናኝ፣ አስተማሪና አሳዛኝ ገጠመኞች ጋር* (Woldeamanuel Gudisso. 2015. The Youth and *Khat*: With Entertaining, Instructive and Sad Anecdotes). 2nd Printing. Far East Trading Printers. Addis Ababa).

Annexes

Annex One: Glossary of Local Terms

Aba Č'äbsi: Oromiffa denoting a *Khat* plant breaker, a thief who steals *Khat* from plantations.

Afosha: *Indigenous voluntary association established primarily to provide mutual aid during burial and mourning matters and sometimes also to address other community concerns. In Harar, the term is used to denote such associations of the Moslem community.*

Aterera: *Offshoots or buds one picks and holds together in the palm, or in small plastic bags, envelops, etc., ready for chewing and then pops directly into the mouth.*

Aräqe: Also known as *Katikala;* is a pure grain, traditional home-distilled beverage that is made from an assortment of cereals such as wheat, sorghum and maize.

Aräqe bet: A tavern specializing in the sale of *Aräqe.*

Bä Sine-Srat Qami: One who chews *Khat* with discipline instead of abuse, with modesty in terms of place chosen, time allocated and amount consumed.

Bärč'a: The act of ceremoniously/leisurely chewing Khat in groups.

Bärč'a-bet: A room dedicated to *Bärč'a,* could also refer to a *Bärč'a* bar that is also called *Khat-bet.*

Č'at: The Institute of Ethiopian Study's official transliteration of the word *Khat* that is used in this work for the benefit of the international readership.

Č'äbsi: From the Oromiffa for "break," *Č'äbsi* is the term that references the substance or activity that is "used" to "break" a *Merqana* so that one can sleep; commonly *Č'äbsi* means the drinking of alcohol, but some Moslems instead drink milk or juice; similarly, manual labor, extended prayer, or some sort of focused study also "breaks" a *Merqana,* though owing to the word's association with alcohol these meanings are sometimes invoked jokingly.

Dukak: *Khat* withdrawal symptom. Torturous nightmares experienced by addicts who go to sleep without chewing their habitual *Khat* and therefore suffer from shortage of breathe. According to the narration of persons that have experienced it, the *Khat* serving that has been skipped comes to them in their dreams to take revenge by interrogating and punishing them in all sorts of strange ways such as dangling them by the hair from the edge of a cliff, etc.

Gäraba: *Khat* leftovers, leaves and branches which are not chewed by most people, but rather discarded because they are too hard, tough and/or dry; In Harar there are homeless (some of whom are obviously mentally ill) who wander house to house collecting *Gäraba* because they cannot afford to buy *Khat;* obviously this "service" is appreciated by the well-to-do chewers who are spared of their waste disposal.

Hawza: Hot beverage made by boiling *Khat* leaves in water the same way tea is brewed, hence also called '*Khat* tea'.

Hagäräsebkät: An Ethiopian Tewahedo Orthodox Church ecclesiastic administrative area that covers a region, Diocese.

Haram: Referring to acts that are forbidden by Allah, and one of Five Islamic Commandments that define the morality of human action.

Harara: Acute craving for *Khat*. The psychological condition experienced by a habitual chewer who hasn't chewed *Khat;* some people state that it makes people short-tempered, angry or aggressive; but its intensity is said to vary from person to person

Hambis: Oromiffa for one who is "possessed" or "captured" by *Khat*

Hailäña Suss: Strong addiction.

Ïddïr: Funerary association. Voluntary association established primarily to provide mutual aid during burial and mourning events, and sometimes also to address other community concerns. In Harar, the term is used to denote such associations formed by non-Moslems.

Ïqqub: Rotating saving and credit association that lasts for the duration of a single round of benefit distribution, unless renewed.

Ijja bana: Oromiffa, meaning eye opener, and name given to a small serving of *Khat* that is taken as soon as one wakes up n order to reactivate one's system

Isser: Small *Khat* bundle that is traded in retail business in Assosa.

Jämbe: A load or stack (Amharic *Shäkem*) of about 1.5 Quintal used in *Khat* wholesale trading in Assosa.

Jäzba:	One who chews *Khat* morning, afternoon and night, does not think about work and neglects himself, and others, etc.; in popular description, one who would not care as long as he got more *Khat*; sometimes also known by its more all-purpose Amharic synonym of *Näfäz*.
Käbad Suss:	Heavy addiction.
Khat, Č'at:	(*Catha edulis*) *Khat*, also known as *Chat, Qat, Gaad, Miraa, etc.*, a stimulant mostly used as unprocessed recreational drug, commonly chewed, and sometimes imbibed after it has been pounded into a mush in a *Muqecha*.
Mahbär:	Traditional club-like association of about a dozen or so persons organized to meet, celebrate, and bond around a certain religious figure that is common among Ethiopian Tewahedo Orthodox Christians.
Mahbere-Qidusan:	A well-established and influential youth wing of the ETOC with chapters in almost all of the country's cities and universities as well as abroad.
Makär:	The process by which *Khat* stalks are laid lengthwise and tied together into bundles of varying size after reaping; a task that is usually the exclusive work domain of unfortunate children and youth
Mädäb:	A spot at home that is specially assigned to *Bärč'a or Khat* chewing.
Mäqam:	The act of picking offshoots and popping them directly into the mouth.
Marana:	The resultant "high" of chewing *Khat:* it refers to the physical and mental condition induced by *Khat's* active ingredients. The nature of *Merqana* varies from person to person
Mäshruf:	Pocket money that is provided for the specific purpose of purchasing *Khat*.
Muqecha:	Mortar for pounding leaves into a mush; during this process a little water is added to the leaves being crushed and, if the imbiber so desires, so is a little sugar; the mixture is then consumed in one of two ways; if the user is a chewer and wants something in his/her mouth, he or she will eat it with a spoon; or, if the user does not want to chew anything, he or she will mix it with water and drink the concoction; this latter method is most common among older

persons who have lost teeth and can no longer chew as effectively (if at all) as they once could.

Shisha: A syrupy tobacco-mix containing molasses and vegetable glycerol which is smoked in a hookah. Typical flavors include apple that has a strong aniseed flavor, grape, guava, lemon, mint, as well as many other fruit based mixes.

Tinat-bet: An Amharic term meaning 'study room', which euphemistically refers to *Bärč'a room*.

Udu Bana: Oromiffa for 'bottom opener' referring to a serving of *Khat* that is taken early in the morning in order to help activate intestinal system and be able to relieve oneself.

Wäräda : District. The middle-level state administrative unit (with an elected council) lying between Regional State and *Qäbäle (Kebele)*, and placed under the Zone for coordination purposes.

Wäta-Gäba Bay: An "on-and-off" or infrequent *Khat* user. One that is not yet captured by or dependent on *Khat*

Yä Č'at Suss: *Khat* addiction. Being dependent on regular *Khat* consumption.

Yä Č'at Amäl: *Khat* habit. Being in the habit of regular *Khat* consumption; a term that signifies a lesser level of attachment as compared to *Yä Č'at Suss*.

Yä izin: Food and/or drinks brought to a house of mourning by kin, friends, neighbors, and particularly fellow *iddïr* members.

Annex Two: Resolution of the 22nd Annual Conference of the Ethiopian Public Health Association (EPHA) on Alcohol, Substance, *Khat* and Tobacco

Preamble

Recognizing the alarming nature of the public health problem that stems from excessive and unwarranted use of alcohol, substance, *Khat* and tobacco, with a high adverse impact particularly on the youth of the Nation;

Reviewing the legal and socio-economic dimensions of the problem by means of awareness creation campaigns, stimulating public concerns and engaging in active discussions through the mass media;

Working closely with and soliciting the support of relevant Government organs and stakeholders such as the United States Centre for Disease Control (CDC), the Canadian Public Health Association (CPHA) and the Framework Convention Alliance (FCA) over the past two years;

Conducting a successful mass walk in Addis Ababa on the 30th of October 2011 along with Save Your Generation Ethiopia (SYGE) as a pre-conference event;

The Ethiopian Public Health Association (EPHA), after listening to and deliberating upon study findings and experiences of renowned experts in the area presented to its 22nd Annual Conference held on the 1st to 3rd of November 2011 at the United Nations Conference Centre (UNCC) in Addis Ababa, has noted that:

- Much needs to be done to bring about awareness and concern amongst the general public, policy makers, legislators and law enforcement organs;
- The rate of consumption of these hazardous substances is increasingly on the rise from year to year;
- Both in and out of school youths are the most affected and vulnerable group; Secondary schools and higher learning institutions are becoming hot spots of the problem;
- Ethiopia is not only a hub for trafficking these substances through its ports of entry and exit (airports, adjacent seaports, postal services) but it has also become a major producer and consumer of these substances;

- The geographic distribution of production and consumption of these harmful substances has widened during the past few decades; so much so that even parts of the country which were not known to have the problem are now becoming important centers of production, distribution and consumption;
- Alcohol, substance, *Khat* and tobacco predispose the youth to risky sexual behaviors and increase the risk of disposition to HIV and other STIs and unwanted pregnancy, which in-turn contribute to reduced school performance and work efficiency;
- Alcohol, substance, *Khat* and tobacco are not only limited to their immediate consequences, but are major causes of chronic non-communicable complications such as cardiovascular diseases, diabetics and chronic respiratory diseases;
- The policy and legal environment governing the excessive use of alcohol, tobacco and the like to protect the public are lax, incomplete or non-existent;
- There are no adequate and readily accessible counseling and rehabilitation services for those affected by the problem; and
- There is a lack of systematically organized data collection and use of existing evidence on the problem that can inform policy formulation and help in designing intervention measures and strategies.

The conference also noted that the responsibility for getting rid of the adverse consequences of alcohol, substances, *Khat* and tobacco falls not only on the health sector but equally on the family, civil society organizations, religious leaders, the education system (public and private), the media, all socio-economic sectors and ultimately on each of us and particularly the youth.

In view of the above and encouraged by the request forwarded in the opening address of the State Minister of Health of the Federal Democratic Republic of Ethiopia to convey the outcome of the deliberations of the Conference to his Ministry, it is hereby resolved as follows.

Resolution

1. Increase awareness and concern of policy makers/ legislators, law enforcement agencies and the larger public including the youth on the adverse consequences of alcohol, substance, *Khat* and tobacco on a sustainable basis.

2. Enact and strengthen laws and regulations that would be instrumental in protecting the wider public from the adverse consequences of alcohol and substances abuse by:

    a. Specifying the minimum legal age for alcohol sale and consumption.

    b. Expediting ratification of the WHO Framework Convention on Tobacco Control (FCTC).

    c. Prohibiting the consumption and distribution in any form of alcohol substance and tobacco use in public places like schools, health facilities and work places.

    d. Banning advertisements of alcohol and tobacco through the means of the mass media.

3. Strengthen and expand service facilities to provide counselling, psychosocial support and treatment, rehabilitation and other services for people affected by the problem.

4. Strengthen systematically organized data collection through operational research and the use of available evidence on the problem that can inform policy formulation and intervention means.

5. Use every opportunity to teach and publicize the adverse consequences especially in the curriculum development and training of health services.

6. Look for alternative income generation schemes for those who are dependent for their livelihood in the production and distribution of the harmful substances as a long-term solution.

7. Establish/strengthen existing multi-sectoral national forums to monitor and follow up the implementation of activities intended to get rid of the adverse consequences of these detrimental substances.

The General Assembly of the EPHA finally recommended that this Resolution be submitted to the Federal Ministry of Health (FMoH) and other relevant organs including the House of Peoples' Representatives, Ministry of Justice (MoJ), Ministry of Labor and Social Affairs (MoLSA), Ministry of Education (MoE), Ministry of Women, Children and Youth Affairs (MoWCY), Ministry of Trade (MoT), Ministry of Science and Technology (MoST), Ministry of Federal Affairs (MoFA), and Ministry of Government Communications (MoGC) for their appropriate actions and decisions.

The Conference further entrusted the Executive Board and Secretariat of the EPHA with the responsibility of collaborating with the Government, sister professional associations, other civil society organizations (CSOs) and all concerned in the realization of this Resolution.

EPHA's 22nd Annual Conference

United Nations Conference Centre (UNCC)

Addis Ababa, Ethiopia

Annex Three: Symbols used for the Transliteration of Ethiopian Words

Vowel	Symbol	Example	
1st order	ä	ዘፈነ	Zäffänä
2nd order	u	ሁሉ	hullu
3rd order	i	ሂድ	hid
4th order	a	ራራ	rarra
5th order	e	ቤት	bet
6th order	ï	እግር	ïgïr
7th order	o	ሆድ	hod

~~~~~ ≡ ≡ ≡ ≡ ≡ ~~~~~

Consonant	Symbol	Example	
ሽ	š	ሽሽ	šäššä
ቅ	q	ቆቅ	qoq
ች	č	ቸረቸረ	čäräččärä
ኝ	ñ	ኞኞ	ñoñño
ዥ	ž	ጋዥ	gäž
ይ	y	ይታይ	yïttay
ጅ	j	ጀግና	jägna
ጥ	t́	ጠጣ	t́ät́ta
ጭ	č'	ተንጫጫ	tänč'ač'č'a
ጵ	p'	ጳውሎስ	P'awlos
ጽ	s'	ጸሰት	s'äs'ät
ምgʷ	mʷa	ልምgʷ	lmʷa

Source: Journal of Ethiopian Studies (JES).